Mary —

The book we
could have / should have
written long ago!

Jeanne

2007

Down, Boy!

Down, Boy!

A Girl's Guide
to Housebreaking a Man

Lisa Hamilton

**Andrews McMeel
Publishing**

Kansas City

Down, Boy!

ISBN: 0-7407-4184-5

Library of Congress Control Number: 2003112913

04 05 06 07 08 TWP 10 9 8 7 6 5 4 3 2 1

Book design by Holly Camerlinck

Attention: Schools and Businesses

Andrews McMeel books are available at quantity discounts with bulk
purchase for educational, business, or sales promotional use. For information,
please write to: Special Sales Department, Andrews McMeel Publishing,
4520 Main Street, Kansas City, Missouri 64111.

For

Max

Contents

FIVE

Basic Training: Boot Camp for Boyfriends . . . 77

SIX

Why Won't My Boyfriend Listen to Me?
Establishing Communication Right from the Start . . . 89

SEVEN

"Get Off My Leg!" Sex and Your Boyfriend . . . 103

EIGHT

Housebreaking 101:
Bringing Home a New Boyfriend . . . 117

NINE

Sit Up, Boy! Exercising, Feeding,
and Grooming Your Boyfriend . . . 133

Acknowledgments

I would like to thank my agent, P. J. Mark, whose great advice and humorous additions shaped the book. Patty Rice and Lillian Ruggles were the nicest editors ever. Julie Hilden and Stephen Glass were incredibly supportive and enthusiastic readers, Alex Smithline offered sartorial advice, and Gail Furman provided a great "writer's retreat" on Long Island. The book was enhanced by all my female friends who shared their own training tips and by all the boyfriends who needed them.

Introduction

Women love their dogs, and they love their boyfriends. But both dogs and boyfriends sometimes need a little extra training to be a satisfying life companion.

In the 1962 movie *If a Man Answers,* Sandra Dee plays rich, perky socialite Chantal Stacy. When her mother wants to help Sandra/Chantal manage her man (played by Bobby Darin), she gives her daughter a dog-training manual for reference. As usual, mother knows best: You *can* train your man, just like you train your dog!

Down, Boy! is a comprehensive training manual for men. It offers golden rules for relationships on the assumption that we like, or even love, men—maybe even as much as we love dogs.

If a woman is boyfriend shopping, *Down, Boy!* provides a helpful guide to the different types of boyfriends and their traits. And if she already has a problem boyfriend, this book will help her make the adjustments necessary to turn him into woman's best friend, instead of having to put up with an annoying pest, because it's important to have a well-trained life companion. Suggestions are tailored to the types of boyfriend, because there is no one-size-fits-all solution to your boyfriend problems!

Down, Boy!

ONE

So, You Want to Get a Boyfriend!

Getting a new boyfriend can be the beginning of years of happiness, and the bond between a woman and her boyfriend can exceed even the greatest of expectations. To ensure that you have the best relationship with your boyfriend, you must be prepared for some important responsibilities. Having a boyfriend is a lifestyle choice, and before making it you should take stock of all aspects of your life.

AM I READY FOR A BOYFRIEND?
A Quick Quiz

Keep the following questions in mind as you search for the perfect boyfriend.

1. How will I find the right boyfriend to fit into my lifestyle and home?

It's important to maintain a high level of self-awareness and a clear understanding of what you are looking for in a boyfriend. A woman who likes to sleep late on the weekends shouldn't get a boyfriend who is up, alert, and needing to go out at the crack of dawn.

2. Will I have enough time and patience to spend training, grooming, and exercising a boyfriend?

Boyfriends are a big time commitment. While they may seem cute, cuddly, and endlessly entertaining at first, they can become a more serious responsibility as the relationship progresses. If you think you might not have the time for a full-time commitment, consider spending time with someone else's boyfriend on the weekends.

3. Am I willing to spend the resources to ensure the best future for a boyfriend?

Boyfriends aren't cheap. In addition to time, it costs money to care for one. That beginning-of-relationship shopping spree, when you re-dress them from head to toe, will cost you. And it's not just the upfront costs like the new wardrobe: It's a lifetime of Christmas presents,

birthday bashes, and springing for that occasional weekend out of town. Do the math now, so that you don't
end up several years into the relationship with a boyfriend
you can no longer afford to keep. There is nothing sad-
der than having to give him away to a better home
because of poor financial planning on your part.

4. *Do I have the patience to keep a boyfriend?*
When dealing with a new boyfriend, especially when you
first bring him into the house, you need to be willing to
overlook mistakes and accidents with grace, and without
raising your voice or making any sudden, scary gestures.
For example, if the boyfriend's sweating beer bottle leaves a
ring on your newly painted coffee table, it's best not to
yell, but to instead, in a firm voice, making steady eye contact, say, "No beers on the coffee table, darling." The same
method should be used when he puts his feet on the furniture, consistently arrives late for your dates, or thinks that
carnations are an acceptable flower to send you.

5. *Am I willing to forgo other activities to take care of
and spend time with a boyfriend?*
Your boyfriend will look to you for all of his emotional
needs, and many of his physical ones, so you must be

prepared to make personal sacrifices (not seeing other men, seeing less of your female friends) while you establish a bond with your new boyfriend. Eventually, he will be trained and self-sufficient, and you can begin to integrate him into your activities, or at least feel secure enough to leave him at home alone on Saturday nights with a video if you have something better to do.

The Benefits of Boyfriend Ownership

Boyfriends can be loving companions if properly trained and cared for. Once they become part of the family, you will be rewarded with years of devotion. The mental health benefits associated with boyfriend ownership include lowered stress levels and an improved outlook on life.

Jane, twenty-eight, lives in Chicago. Although she has a small apartment, she feels that she is ready to make the commitment to owning a boyfriend. "On weekend afternoons, it would be nice to have someone to go running with," Jane says. "Three months ago, I met my boyfriend at a friend's party. I've never been happier. I've had to make some sacrifices, but he's always there when I need him. He's a loyal, wonderful companion."

Jane's friend, Hillary, isn't so sure that Jane's boyfriend will always remain so loyal and wonderful, but she admits that Jane has never seemed happier. "She has that sparkle in her eyes," says Hillary. "And it's been good for her to have someone to 'exercise' with."

Other women praise the convenience of boyfriends who have been properly trained in the "fetch" command.

"I hate having to go and get my newspaper in the mornings," says Kara, who lives in a fourth floor walk-up in New York's East Village. "But my boyfriend, he's one of those early-rising, energetic types. He's out the door and getting me the Times, a coffee, and a muffin. It's fabulous."

Some owners get to feel the warm fuzzies of transforming the life of a boyfriend for the better.

"When I met my boyfriend, he was living in the city, never got any fresh air, never got to romp in the outdoors," says Sarah, twenty-nine, a resident of Missoula, Montana. "He moved to my ranch in Montana with me, and he's like a whole different boyfriend. Much happier, much healthier, and he's lost that nervous scratching habit he had when he was an investment banker. He's happy, and that makes me happy."

The Drawbacks of Boyfriend Ownership

Some experts caution women about getting a boyfriend just because their friends have one, or because they see media images of particular boyfriends.

"I was watching a movie starring Hugh Grant, and I thought, 'I want one of those British boyfriends,'" says Kelly, thirty-two, of Santa Monica, California. "So I started hanging around at a British pub near my house, and met my ex-boyfriend. Sure, those British men are cute onscreen, but have you ever really dealt with some of them close up? He was always running off to the pub and drinking with his 'mates,' and he thought that beans on toast constituted a meal. But the worst thing was the hygiene problem. There's just a different standard in Europe, I think, or maybe he was just lazy. But he was no Hugh Grant."

Kelly's problem was that she jumped into boyfriend ownership by basing her decision on a boyfriend she'd seen in the movies. The reality can often be very different and disillusioning. Entering into a relationship with a boyfriend too quickly or neglecting to ask yourself the important questions about your own preparedness can result in having to abandon a boyfriend, or at least to endure years of irritation before provoking him into running away.

"A bad relationship with a boyfriend can just ruin your whole day," says Boston resident Cintra, twenty-seven. "I mean, you wake up in the morning, he's there, pestering you. I had a needy boyfriend, and I didn't have the time to

give him what he wanted. I ended up pretend-
ing we were going on a beach vacation, and
driving him out to Cape Cod and leaving him in
front of the drive-in movie at Wellfleet. I fig-
ured someone would find him there and let him
get into their car. I just couldn't handle it any
more. It was heartbreaking to leave him like
that, but I had no other choice."

Old Dogs or New Tricks?

Once you've resolved to get a boyfriend, deciding what
kind is the next step. First, you need to decide whether
you want a younger or older boyfriend.

With an older man (say, thirty-five-plus in human
years), what you see is what you get. Adult men have
reached maturity, and their personality is often set,
although many of their learned behavior and attitudes can
be altered with careful training.

One of the positive things about an older boyfriend
is precisely his maturity level and the experience he

brings to a relationship. Adult men are often more stable than younger men.

> "My new boyfriend is forty. Before that, I'd dated this twenty-five-year-old who had lots of energy, but was a little dumb," says Jennifer, thirty-three. "My older boyfriend, while he may have had a few bad habits, is able to act calmly and rationally in tense situations, and can fall back on his life experience to solve problems. The younger one just got too hyper and seemed often to be chasing his tail instead of confronting problems head on."

Depending on their previous experiences with other women, older men are perhaps more set in their ways, and may be distrustful or jaded because of abusive relationships with past mistresses.

WHAT TO EXPECT FROM OLD DOGS

He will be set in his ways, so give him some time to adjust.

Learning the personality of a new mistress and her new rules and boundaries will take longer. If his last mistress was abusive or hard to take, he may be damaged and averse to gentle correction.

Don't tolerate the bad habits he picked up in earlier relationships.

Observe the adult man's bad habits and then plan and initiate a corrective or reeducation program immediately. The earlier you make clear that he should not drool all over your clothes, the better.

Older men absorb new rules more quickly than a younger boyfriend.

Their maturity level is higher, their attention span is longer, and they are probably already familiar with some of the basic commands; for example, if you ask them to "fetch," you are likely to be rewarded with flowers or jewelry.

Remember, some bad habits are hard to break!

You may want to think about the fact that your new boyfriend's unacceptable behavior may be ingrained and require a great deal of time and effort to be eradicated. Once a toilet-seat splatterer, always a seat splatterer. . . .

> Lea, thirty-six, has an older boyfriend whose ingrained habits are giving her pause. "Older men are set in their ways and they have routines that are hard to change. My boyfriend also has issues from his ex-wife that are proving difficult to overcome. I'm starting to understand why his first marriage failed."

> Another woman with an older boyfriend, Paula, thirty-two, complains, "My older boyfriend is just so neurotic because of his past abuse that he acts out in public, peeing in corners on the street and barking into his cell phone. I just don't know what to do with him sometimes."

If you think you might grow tired of having to work this hard, consider a blank slate: a younger man. Younger boyfriends are a challenge and an adventure.

They are cuddly and adorable and easy to bond with. Within days of meeting you, they will quickly begin to follow you around, getting underfoot and rarely going far from you. However, these adorable creatures have their drawbacks as well.

WHAT TO EXPECT FROM PUPPIES

Endless "play" behavior.

Petting, wrestling, and other kinds of romps are fun for a while, but may get boring as you want more from the relationship. You may enjoy those all-day make-out sessions for a little while, but eventually he'll wear you out.

It might be awhile before your younger boyfriend is ready for a fully adult relationship.

Are you willing to wait until he's stopped chasing his tail or running around after squirrels for him to grow up? Make sure you know what you want out of life before getting involved with a younger boyfriend.

Younger boyfriends have short attention spans.

You may compete for their time and energy with MTV and televised sports, as well as with other women.

Training times may be longer and more tedious since there has been little or no prior training for most of them.

Unlike older boyfriends, younger boyfriends may have no idea where to buy flowers, where to get their clothing dry-cleaned, or how to please women. You will need to teach them *everything*.

Younger boyfriends can get in all kinds of trouble.

They will do things that you may not anticipate: run off, disappear at strange hours to play with their friends, and destroy the furniture.

Ingrid, thirty-four, swears by the (much) younger boyfriend. "What can I say? I have this one little surfer boyfriend, and he can wag his tail for hours. Yummy." While Ingrid may not have anything to say to her little surfer, she does not feel that talking is the most important component of their relationship.

Where to Find a Boyfriend

Where is the best place to find a boyfriend? Bars?
Church? AA meetings? Match.com? Is your boyfriend a
rescue boyfriend or a pedigreed one?

Friends

Friends are almost always the best source of boyfriends,
but make sure they know what you want. They may try
to surprise you with the "gift" of a new boyfriend, by
bringing him to a Christmas party, or for your birthday.
They should be sure that you are ready for the serious
responsibilities inherent in such a gift. A boyfriend is not
a toy.

Rescues

There are two types of rescues: abused and abandoned
boyfriends, and those you "rescue" from others.
Sometimes, an entirely inappropriate woman has a
boyfriend who should be your boyfriend. You, therefore,
are entitled to "rescue" him from his current situation in
order to introduce him to a much happier home. Of

course, sometimes this other woman has no idea about
what an unhappy situation she is forcing on your future
boyfriend, so desperate measures may be necessary. In
other cases, a sad, recently dumped boyfriend can be rescued by you and made to forget his troubles.

Weddings

Weddings are one of the most popular hook-up sites—
you're usually nicely dressed, drunk, and sometimes in
possession of a hotel room. Even men are affected by the
sentimentality of the situation, but, more importantly,
may feel desperation, especially if they are single and
slightly older men; they might suddenly realize their life
is slipping away from them and they are all alone. This is
when you pounce.

Pedigree mills

College, graduate school, alumni association meetings,
and other professional events are a good way of ensuring
that you will meet a boyfriend who has the best possible
background, a boyfriend with "papers." You are generally
assured that the nice doctor or MBA that you meet at
such events will have the earning potential that you may
desire. However, keep in mind that pedigreed boyfriends

may suffer from the effects of inbreeding or from too many years in the Ivy League.

Personal ads

These popular outlets must be used with careful attention to the principle of *caveat emptor,* or "Let the buyer beware." Women seeking a boyfriend through ads or the Internet should be forewarned: Boyfriends acquired this way come with no vetting by friends and may prove to be completely unknown quantities as to temperament and breeding. But given the ubiquity of such avenues of introduction, they cannot be discounted as an important source of potential boyfriends. Just don't be surprised if that six foot two blond is actually five foot six, bald, delusional about his general level of attractiveness, and pees a little when he gets excited.

Laundromats and grocery stores

These are great places to meet boyfriends because of the wealth of information you can glean from their behavior. How domestic is he? Does he properly sort whites from colors? Does he wear tiny, strangely patterned briefs, or the more acceptable boxers? Does he eat a healthy diet?

Does he go gourmet or is his cart overloaded with ramen noodles, frozen pizza, and canned food made with meat by-products of uncertain origin? Does he hoard food or growl when you and he both reach for the last box of cookies? This kind of information might otherwise take a few dates to establish, but if you catch a potential boyfriend in the middle of these tasks, you can avoid a mistake early on—no more discovering that he is a secret slob weeks into the relationship if you've already seen the care he takes getting his socks clean.

Bars and clubs

These places are meet/meat markets, and are often populated by men who are not looking to be your boyfriend. They are best utilized for those between-boyfriend experiences, when you want to meet someone to share a quick romp in the . . . park.

Once you've decided whether or not you're ready to have a boyfriend and pinpointed the kinds of places you are most likely to find or adopt him, you are ready to proceed to a more in-depth discussion of the major boyfriend groups.

Elizabeth Taylor's Master Class

Elizabeth Taylor has earned the dubious distinction of being the only woman alive who has married a man from every "group." *Down, Boy!* therefore defers to her and her vast store of knowledge about all things male—who else has had such varied experience?

It's also useful to note that, after marrying seven men and dating powerful men such as Howard Hughes, she has forgone writing a traditional kiss-and-tell biography about her romances and instead wrote a 2002 book called *My Love Affair with Jewelry.* Liz knows what's important in the end!

Liz married devil-may-care hotel heir Nicky Hilton, a confirmed **Toy** boy, when she was eighteen and divorced him nine months later. Nicky was cute, young, and irresponsible, but he was a good "starter" husband for those young and carefree years.

Miss Taylor was then married to older British actor Michael Wilding, with whom she had two children. Wilding, though involved with entertainment,

was actually a stable human being and therefore probably a **Mixed Breed**.

One of the great loves of her life, next to Richard
Burton and her jewelry, was theater and film producer
Mike Todd, with whom Liz had a brief but satisfying
marriage until his death in a plane crash. He was all
man, a cigar-chomping, plane-flying type who pro-
duced the film *Around the World in Eighty Days,* and he
therefore qualifies as an honorary **Sporting** guy.

Shortly after his funeral, Liz took up with their
best friend, Eddie Fisher, stealing him away from
America's Sweetheart, Debbie Reynolds, and earning
the wrath of the press and the public. Eddie is a fascinating mix: He clearly displayed some **Toy**-like lapdog
qualities in letting himself be transferred from one
mistress to another so easily, but there may be some
Hound complications lurking there as well—Liz was
all sultry sexuality, while Debbie was only cute.
Fisher's public image, up to that point, had been pure
Mixed Breed. He's a perfect example of how it's
sometimes hard to tell what group your boyfriend
might belong to, given that he may possess some red-
herring traits of a different group.

Liz's longtime love and two-time husband Richard Burton was practically a poster boy for the **Hound** group. After breaking up the Fisher-Reynolds marriage, La Liz had no compunction about leaving Fisher for Burton. Their turbulent marriage, his hard-drinking ways, and the huge "Burton-Taylor diamond"—sixty-nine carats!—that he bought her, all add up to *fabulous,* and totally dysfunctional. You can catch scenes from their marriage in the 1966 film *Who's Afraid of Virginia Woolf?*

Liz's six-year marriage to **Terrier** politician John Warner, later Senator Warner, was rumored to have helped his political career. (Taylor was subsequently engaged to another **Terrier,** a Mexican attorney named Victor Luna, but they never married.)

Elizabeth's last husband, whom she met during a 1987 stay at the Betty Ford clinic for painkiller addiction, was a classic **Working** type: construction-equipment operator Larry Fortensky, a man twenty years her junior with a junior-high education. Though their marriage lasted only five years, in marrying him Liz undoubtedly gained insight into drywall, truck pulls, and that complicated, '70s-era feathered hairdo he sported. Never underestimate the bonds formed in rehab, but never make a decision when you are withdrawing from your pill addiction.

In her later years, Miss Taylor has retreated into a close relationship with cross-gendered manchild Michael Jackson, thereby choosing to end her string of liaisons with the opposite sex by pursuing a person whose gender identity is a total cipher. Liz has moved beyond men entirely into the realm of fantasy and fond reminiscences about her jewelry collection. Perhaps that's the only place to go once you have exhausted all the other possibilities. . . .

ASK Elizabeth Taylor

Dear Elizabeth: I'm a single girl in my early thirties and it's been a while since I've had a boyfriend. But I'm busy with my career and worry that if I get a boyfriend and leave him home alone too often, he'll get lonely, act out, and destroy the furniture. During my last relationship, I had a perfectly good couch destroyed by a bored, lonely boyfriend. What should I do?

Perplexed in Parsippany

Elizabeth says: You certainly need to be sure that you have time for a boyfriend and a career. I never let my marriages get in the way of my film career, but you should try to bring some balance into your life. You don't want to wake up at forty and realize that all the cute, young boyfriends are taken and that your only chance is with an older, "rescue" boyfriend, although I did find Larry late in life. Get one while you're still young and can have the pick of the litter. As for time considerations, try to leave work as early as possible, call home to talk to him as much as possible—even if he just hears your voice on the answering machine it's effective—and remember, when you're old, it won't be your job you'll remember fondly, it will be the big, sad eyes of your cute and cuddly boyfriend.

Dear Elizabeth: I've recently had trouble meeting new boyfriends. I just moved to a big city from a small college town, and while I see potential boyfriends everywhere I go, I'm worried about approaching strange boyfriends in public. What should I do?

Bashful in Boston

Elizabeth says: It's wise to be careful when you first approach an unfamiliar potential boyfriend. You don't know how friendly he is or whether he has been properly trained in off-leash behavior. Approach him slowly, make eye contact, and smile. If he does not act aggressively, it's okay to proceed. If you're in a coffee shop or some other casual situation, try to make conversation about something in your common environment: the slowness of the line you're both waiting in, the strange piercings on the counter clerk, or some other innocuous topic. If you're at a work event or more formal situation, try to have someone introduce you. You can tell if he's interested by whether or not he makes and maintains extended eye contact and whether he accepts your friendly overtures. If he growls or is stand-offish, don't persist—move on, because there are always more where he came from.

Dear Elizabeth: I recently met a potential boyfriend with no tags—nothing that signified that he belonged to anyone else. He was wandering alone in the park near my house, and when I stopped to talk to him to see who he belonged to, he didn't mention anyone. I started seeing him, but I just discovered he's owned by another woman! Of course I stopped seeing him, but how can I prevent this from happening in the first place?

Annoyed in Atlanta

Elizabeth says: It was very naughty of him to pretend to be available, but you can't trust some boyfriends.

Learn to spot the signs of a boyfriend who already has an owner: Even if he's not wearing a collar, tags, rings, or other identifying markers, there are signs that he's a kept man. Are his clothes suspiciously stylish and well-coordinated? Are there any buttons missing from his clothes, or are they mended and well-cared-for? Does he have the glow of health? Is he freshly bathed and shaven? A nicely dressed man alone in a coffee shop or at a park may attract your attention, but you should be careful and thoroughly investigate where he lives, what he does, and whether his shots are current, to ensure that he can be adopted by you without problem.

TWO

Hound, Terrier, or Toy?
Choosing the Right Boyfriend for You

The Major Boyfriend Groups

Is there a certain kind of man you have had your eye on, or are you confused about how to select a boyfriend? Here's how to pick the right boyfriend for you, one that will fit in with your lifestyle, your friends, and your family.

The bonus of selecting a purebred boyfriend is his predictability in size, appearance, care requirements, and temperament. Knowing what your cute thirty-year-old boyfriend will look like and the kind of care he will need later in life is key in selecting the breed for you.

The Sporting Group

This group is made up of two of the most recognizable categories of men: preppies and jocks. Since they are naturally active and alert, **Sporting** boyfriends make likable, well-rounded companions. Members of this group can include such diverse sub-breeds as professional athletes, weekend golfers, men who played football in college, men who shoot hoops with their friends, men who consider Foosball and pool sports, avid sports fans, and men who merely wear team paraphernalia. Some are remarkable in their affinity for the outdoors and their survival instincts, and many of them actively continue to participate in athletics and other field activities. Potential girlfriends of **Sporting** boyfriends need to realize that most require regular, invigorating exercise, and are advised that they may be required to participate in sporting activities themselves or at least appear to care about them.

Top occupations of the Sporting group:
High-school football coach, investment banker, insurance sales,
upper-middle management

Top places to meet members of the Sporting group:
The gym, sports bars, the country club, the golf course

Celebrity members of the Sporting group:
George W. Bush, Tiger Woods, Derek Jeter, Bobby Knight

Some specific breeds found in the Sporting group:
WASPs, senators, the Kennedys

The Hound Group

Boyfriends in the **Hound** group may have soulful stares
and big, beautiful brown eyes, but remember, they were bred
for hunting. They enjoy the chase, but once the chase is
over, they may begin looking for a new challenge. **Hounds**
do not, for obvious reasons, make the best or most devoted
boyfriends. Unless "fixed," they may spend too much time
away from home in pursuit of other activities or other
women. Hillary Clinton, for example, was famously

described as having a hard time keeping her husband, Bill (a notorious *Hound*), "on the porch." These men are found (and should be avoided) in singles' bars everywhere.

Top occupations of the Hound group:
Rock musician, author, actor, agent

Top places to meet members of the Hound group:
Backstage, bars, wet T-shirt contests, AA meetings, MTV Spring Break in Miami, on the set

Celebrity members of the Hound group:
Hugh Grant, Bill Clinton, Steven Tyler, Snoop Dogg, Antonio Banderas

Some specific breeds found in the Hound group:
Paternity-suit defenders, owners of videocameras, Abstract Expressionists

The Working Group

Men who belong to the **Working** group have been bred to perform such jobs as guarding property, providing transportation, building houses, and performing rescues.

They are loyal and dependable. These hunky types have been invaluable assets to society throughout the ages. The fireman, policeman, truck driver, and construction worker are included in this group, to name just a few. Physically fit and quick to learn, these intelligent, capable men make solid companions. Their considerable dimensions and strength, however, make some of the **Working** men unsuitable as boyfriends for the average woman, especially one in a small city apartment. Because of their size, some of these men must be carefully and properly trained and provided with lots of space to work and exercise. There are, however, a few subgroups in the **Working** group who are not so big, and whose labor is not manual, but intellectual.

Top occupations of the Working group:
Firefighter, policeman, systems analyst

Top places to meet members of the Working group:
Blue-collar sports bars, the gym, TGI Friday's

Celebrity members of the Working group:
Sebastian Junger, Jesse Ventura, Bill Gates, Jimmy Smits, Mark Wahlberg

Some specific breeds found in the Working group:
Buyers of snowmobiles, ATVs, and sport utility vehicles

The Terrier Group

Women familiar with this group often comment upon the distinctive **Terrier** personality. These are feisty types, who, while not necessarily small, have a tenacious personality that can often make them seem larger than life. They are impatient and usually have little tolerance for the foibles of others. Most make it very clear that they're always eager for a spirited argument. In general, they make engaging boyfriends, but their high spirits and boundless capacity for arguments require women with the determination and patience to tolerate their man's lively character.

Top occupations of the Terrier group:
They are all attorneys, although sometimes they then become high-powered journalists or politicians.

Top places to meet members of the Terrier group:
Fancy restaurants, CNN, court, shul

Celebrity members of the Terrier group:
Chris Matthews, George Stephanopoulos, Alan Dershowitz, Johnnie Cochran

Some specific breeds found in the Terrier group:
NPR listeners, environmentalists, college professors

The Toy Group

The good looks and adorable expressions of **Toy** boys illustrate the main function of this group: arm candy. Don't let their cuteness fool you, though; many **Toys** are tough as nails and hard to please. If you don't buy them Prada for Christmas, you may have seen the last of them. **Toy** boys will always be popular with older women, sophisticated city dwellers without much living space, and women without the desire to commit to a more serious breed. They make ideal playthings and can be terrific "lap" warmers on cold nights. **Toy** breeds often enjoy being taken out to fancy restaurants and stores, where they like being petted and made much of by the saleswomen. However, while members of the **Toy** group are often more interested in each other than in women, this does not diminish their considerable charm as companions.

Top occupations of the Toy group:
Gigolo, hairdresser, shoe salesman, bartender, male model

Top places to meet members of the Toy group:
Swanky restaurants and clubs, Barneys, gay bars

Celebrity members of the Toy group:
All of Joan Collins's husbands, Jann Wenner's boyfriends, and the Calvin Klein underwear models. Also, Leonardo DiCaprio, John Stamos, Alan Cumming, Ricky Martin.

Some specific breeds found in the Toy group:
Club kids, hipsters, men who wear briefs

The Mixed Breed Group

The **Mixed Breed** group is a grab bag of traits and sizes. However, its very eclecticism means that it is often the most likely source of good boyfriends. The lack of an overarching set of common traits means that many men with more pronounced personalities are classified in the other groups, while the average, everyday guy who is not a working, sporting, or toy breed is found here. Here you can meet the nice guy-next-door type: quiet, unassuming, and possibly a little dull.

Top occupations of the Mixed Breed group:
High-school science teacher, computer programmer, minister or rabbi

Top places to meet members of the Mixed Breed group:
Oldies rock concerts, the supermarket, PTA meetings

Celebrity members of the Mixed Breed group:
John Cusack, Benjamin Bratt, Colin Firth, Denzel Washington, Al Gore

Some specific breeds found in the Mixed Breed group:
Jam-band fans, country music fans, men who patronize comedy clubs

Which Group Is Right for You?

Too frequently, common sense goes out the window when it comes to picking the right breed of boyfriend. Acquiring a boyfriend is like acquiring anything else: The more you know before you buy, the better off you will be. We strongly recommend that you spend enough time investigating the characteristics of each before committing. Remember, boyfriends may be for life, not just for the Christmas party.

Always be honest with yourself. The **Toy** boy you fell in love with because of his impeccable linen suits is indeed beautiful, but are you going to be able to afford him in the future? Think about the size of your house or your apartment. Will that giant **Working** man be happy in your studio?

AM I A HOUND "HOUND"? A TERRIER CHASER?

A Quick Quiz

Ask yourself the following questions:

1. How much time do I have to devote to his physical care and grooming?

If your answer is "not much," avoid high-maintenance types like **Toys** and **Terriers**: The **Toys** will always be wanting to visit the Clinique for Men counter at any department store, while a **Terrier's** constantly heightened testosterone level means balding, which often means hair plugs.

2. *Do I like sports? Can I even tolerate watching them on TV?*

If your answer is "No, I would rather poke a sharp stick in my eye than watch televised or live sporting events," be sure to avoid **Sporting** and **Working** groups in particular. Unfortunately for you, many men, even the most unlikely ones (i.e., **Toys**), may harbor a love of one sport or another. It's probably best to learn to tolerate some sports watching, but be sure to gauge exactly how much you might be exposed to.

3. *Am I the jealous type?*

If you can't keep yourself from turning into the green-eyed monster at the slightest provocation, avoid the **Hound** group. These men are the Mick Jaggers of the boyfriend world, always on the lookout for something new to sniff around. They are sexy, but if you get jealous easily, stay with the more open-hearted and honest **Working** or **Mixed Breed** types who, while affectionate with everyone, are most loyal to their mistresses.

4. How much money am I willing to spend on dates with a boyfriend?

The most expensive boyfriends are the **Toys,** of course, whose unorthodox approach to life often leads them to happily expect you to pick up all the checks. **Hounds** may simply drift off in pursuit of something new and "forget" to pay. Other, more reliable groups like the **Working, Mixed Breed,** and **Sporting** men will usually pick up the tab for nights out (at TGI Friday's, the Olive Garden, and ESPN Zone, respectively). **Terriers** will always pick up the check to display their financial security or as a show of domination.

5. What do I like to do on a date?

If you're a social butterfly who loves nightclubs and cultural or intellectual stimulation, it's **Toys, Hounds,** and **Terriers** for you. If you like to take long walks on the beach and go on picnics, look to the sweet and gentle **Mixed Breed** group. For wholesome outdoor activities like baseball games or tennis, **Working** and **Sporting** men are the ones to pick.

WHAT KIND OF OWNER AM I?

— *Another Quick Quiz* —

It's important to know what kind of person you are, since both selecting a boyfriend and training him should be tailored to *your* personality as well as his.

1. *On Saturday, I like to:*
   (a) Spend the day outdoors.
   (b) Hit the sales.

2. *I like camping. I am happy to pee in the woods. Yes or no?*
   (a) Yes, I don't even need toilet paper!
   (b) No, gross. This is why God invented condos.

3. *Going out on Valentine's Day is crucial. Yes or no?*
   (a) No, I'd rather avoid the hassle.
   (b) Yes, darling, of course it is.

4. In the morning, I have to put lipstick on before anyone can look directly at me. Yes or no?

(a) No, I don't even own lipstick.

(b) Yes, I need at least fifteen minutes before I can be seen.

5. I always order salad dressing "on the side."

(a) Why would I do that?

(b) Of course! It's, like, a thousand calories per serving.

6. When I go to the beach, I like to:

(a) Jump right in and go swimming.

(b) Unpack my giant bag and spend twenty minutes applying sunscreen.

7. My parents' nickname for me was

(a) Hey, you!

(b) Princess

8. On a vacation, I'd rather be

(a) Hiking

(b) Spa-ing

9. *My car is a*
 (a) Jeep
 (b) VW Cabriolet

10. *My favorite drink is*
 (a) Beer
 (b) Champagne

All or mostly (a): You are officially "low maintenance." This kind of owner can have a boyfriend who
isn't attuned to her every need or desire. When reading
this book, you should always choose the more straight-
forward, less "manipulative" option for training your
boyfriend. You also may enjoy outdoor or sporting activities and will find your perfect boyfriend among the
Working, Sporting, and **Mixed Breed** groups.

All or mostly (b): You are very "high maintenance." As
an owner, you will require a boyfriend who is used to
advanced obedience work or naturally attuned to the
needs of his mistress. You will naturally gravitate to the
more complicated and demanding methods of boyfriend
training, since you will require a high level of compliance.
You are more interested in cultural activities and are
more compatible with **Hounds, Terriers,** and **Toys.**

ASK
Elizabeth Taylor

Dear Elizabeth: For years I've been dating Hounds, and, boy, in my current relationship, am I tired of waiting up for him when I know perfectly well he is out chasing tail—and not his own tail. I'm attracted to his brooding good looks and the sex is great, but I can't stand his bad behavior any more. What should I do?

Fed Up in Fresno

Elizabeth says: Even Jerry Hall and Liz Hurley knew when to give up on relationships with **Hounds.** With me, it was two marriages to Richard Burton that did it. It's good that you've come to this realization, and what you need to do now is to figure out what other qualities are important to you when it comes to a boyfriend. If you're still looking for the fun of nightlife, consider a **Toy.** If hulking, masculine sexuality is what you want, consider a **Working** boyfriend. For intellectual stimulation, a **Terrier** is your best bet. It's probably too soon to try a **Sporting** boyfriend (too clean-cut) or a **Mixed Breed** (too nice)—because their differences from the **Hounds** you love to hate are too pronounced. Good luck, stay strong, and stay away from those bad-boy **Hounds!** (I can sympathize with your plight. . . .)

Dear Elizabeth: I've been spending time with a Toy for a while, and I just can't tell where this relationship is going to go. He's cute, he's sweet, and we have a great time together shopping and going to the movies, but I sometimes get the feeling his heart's not in it. How can I figure this out?

Confused in Cambridge

Elizabeth says: Ah, this question makes me think fondly of my lovely friend and costar Montgomery Clift. But there's an instructive scene in one of my favorite *newer* movies, the modern classic *Clueless*, in which our heroine Cher Horowitz discovers that she has mistaken the handsome classmate she has a crush on for a heterosexual. Watch that movie and learn: Is he a better dancer than you are? A better dresser? Better versed in art and film history? Does he display little interest in your body but a lot in your designer clothes? I am the first to insist that not all **Toys** are interested only in each other—I did marry Nicky Hilton after all—but the signs are there if you look for them. With a little effort you may be able to find another **Toy** who knows about Prada and Proust, but who will *also* go to bed with you.

Dear Elizabeth: I've just started seeing a Sporting boyfriend. I really adore him—his shiny hair, his bright eyes, and his boundless energy are really attractive. But I'm hopeless at sports! I don't know anything about them. Is there a crash course I can take so I can understand what he's talking about?

Unsporting in Utica

Elizabeth says: I want to warn you not to pretend to be something you're not, because there are a lot of actual female athletes and women who follow sports out there, and you are in competition with them for **Sporting** boyfriends. But it's sweet that you want to share his interests. Try reading the sports page on a regular basis so you know what season it is. When he says he's "watching the game" you'll know whether it's football, basketball, or baseball. And if he's on a coed softball team or some such thing, why not try to play with him? He'll appreciate your effort to spend time with him, but wear something tight, so if you screw up and drop the ball, he might not even notice.

All About Him
Breeding, Kennels, and Pedigree

It's vitally important, when choosing a boyfriend, to know where he came from. Such information can be gathered through a "home visit," first to his home, and later, to that of his parents.

His Home Environment

The boyfriend's own home environment—his kennel—is usually an accurate indicator of his personality traits. Here are some major types of kennels and the breeds that are likely to live in them.

"Cinder block and Halogen lamp" kennels

These house a **Sporting** or **Working** boyfriend who has recently graduated from college and ceased to live in his fraternity house. In addition to cinder block furniture, there is usually a distressed sofa, a giant TV, and a beer-can collection. There will be no clean towels in the bathroom, no toilet paper, and there will be hair in the drain. Never stay overnight at these apartments. These men are young and are to be avoided until you are ready to marry them and commit to intensive retraining, at which point they are the breeds most likely to let you do whatever you want with the decoration of your new house, as long as there is space for the big TV.

Scary Bauhaus kennels

He's either an architect, or gay, or both. Or perhaps European. The extremely trendy and well-tended interior is either a cause for rejoicing or dismay. There are only a few single, straight men in this world who have this taste. You probably need to do more investigating of this one, who is most likely of the **Toy** persuasion.

Arts and Crafts kennels

Few women have ever met a real, live man who has this kind of interior design, but the interesting leading men in movies always have Mission furniture, tastefully framed black-and-white photographs, and clean bedsheets and bath towels in muted, masculine colors. If you actually encounter this creature in reality, capture him immediately.

Sci-fi kennels

Any woman who has ever had sex on Star Wars or Star Trek sheets knows how disturbing it is to wake up staring at Spock or an Ewok. Men with this kind of decor are usually computer geeks or mathematicians, usually part of the **Working** or **Mixed Breed** groups, and are usually amenable to redecoration.

Regular-guy kennels

This is the most common and therefore the hardest to decode for further clues to type. Adult men with decent incomes usually turn to the Crate and Barrel leather collection and a nice wooden headboard, along with such frills as a Bang & Olufsen stereo system and a collection of different single-malt Scotches. This is usually the best you can hope for, even if it is the most generic.

What Does My Boyfriend Do in His Spare Time?

Getting a look at the books that he reads, the movies and TV shows he watches, and the CDs he listens to will provide you with further clues to his type.

WHAT HE READS

Hound

Keeps Foucault's *History of Sexuality* (all three volumes) and Frederic Jameson's *Postmodernism, or the Cultural Logic of Late Capitalism* on view, has *How to Please a Woman Every Time* beside his bed, and copies of *The Paris Review* in his bathroom.

Terrier

His shelves are crammed with legal textbooks, biographies of political figures, and the novels of Henry James. Has *The Story of O* next to his bed and back issues of *The Nation* or *The New Republic* in his bathroom.

Working

Has maybe cracked the spines of a few novels by Elmore Leonard and may have copies of *Introduction to Programming in Basic* (if he's a white-collar *Working* boyfriend). He keeps *Penthouse* in the bathroom.

Mixed Breed

Has purchased a copy of *Men Are from Mars, Women Are from Venus* to try to figure out a previous girlfriend, and has everything by John Grisham and James Patterson. He keeps the Bible next to his bed, but has a *Playboy* hidden under the mattress.

Toy

Has immaculately bound collections of *W*, *Wallpaper*, and *Architectural Digest* on stainless-steel bookshelves, along with novels like Oscar Wilde's *The Picture of Dorian Gray* and *Frisk* by Dennis Cooper. Keeps the poems of A. E. Housman displayed next to his bed, but is actually reading the copy of Jacqueline Susann's *Valley of the Dolls* hidden in the nightstand. Would never read in the bathroom.

Sporting

He has copies of *Esquire*, *Sports Illustrated*, and *Maxim* scattered all over. No books.

WHAT HE WATCHES

Hound

Maintains an impressive collection of kitschy '70s porn DVDs (which he will invite you to view "ironically" with him), and is obsessive about obscure European art films.

Terrier

Watches *The West Wing* religiously and is also fond of all the *Law and Order* reruns on cable. Obsessively TiVos everything, whether or not he plans to watch it.

Working

Loves HBO's *Real Sex* and *Oz* and can usually be found watching FX. Has the complete *Beavis and Butthead* on DVD.

Mixed Breed

Will indulge you by watching *Sex and the City* on occasion, but by himself enjoys the reruns of '80s movies on TBS—he always had a crush on Molly Ringwald.

Toy

Loves *What Not to Wear* on BBC America and has the complete DVD box set of *Ab Fab*. Secretly upset that *Dynasty* isn't showing more frequently in reruns.

Sporting

Subscribes to all the extra satellite sports channels so he can have saturation coverage. Will also tune into *The O'Reilly Factor* and CNBC for practical purposes.

WHAT HE LISTENS TO

Hound

Puts on jazz or Marvin Gaye's *Let's Get It On* to get you in the mood, and the smarter ones may try to impress you with something cerebral like Serge Gainsbourg. When alone, usually listens to Nick Cave and the Bad Seeds or Johnny Cash.

Terrier

Loves Charles Mingus, Gustav Mahler, and Elvis Costello (from his punkish, Angry Young Man period). Also a fan of bands like Sonic Youth and Hüsker Dü from his college days. His CDs are alphabetized, and he will always want to discuss which obscure indie label something was recorded on.

Working

Has Springsteen—all of it—as well as the Rolling Stones, Jon Bon Jovi, or Wilco, depending on his region of origin and educational level. May listen to country music, unironically.

Mixed Breed

Is unembarassed to own *Dancin' to the '80s*, and has the complete oeuvre of U2. Also secretly likes Jewel and even owns her book of poetry. Wants to listen to what you want to listen to.

Toy

It's the Holy Trinity—Madonna, Cher, and Britney—as well as electronica compilations and trendy stuff like Stereolab. Has tabs of E stuck in one of the CD cases.

Sporting

Has a scratched Hootie and the Blowfish CD, loves *The Greatest Stadium Anthems of All Time,* and is devoted to

the Dave Matthews Band. His Walkman is tuned to
classic rock when he works out. May also listen to metal.

Is He the Pick of the Litter?

It's important to meet his parents and check out his
pedigree before doing more than dipping your toe into
their gene pool. The more relatives you meet, the better
an idea you'll have about what your offspring might
look like. Short of pulling back their gums to look at
their teeth, you can still check out health histories and
mental stability through a few well-timed home visits.

Sporting types often come from a family of the
same. Big and healthy, their family centers its activities
around outdoor activities or televised sporting events.
Holidays with the **Sporting** family are convivial affairs
involving a spontaneous touch football game or a particularly spirited game of Charades.

You'll be lucky if you ever meet anyone in the
Hound's family. He will probably be secretive about their
existence, their home address, or any other facts about
them. The most you might hope for with a **Hound** is

seeing a photograph of them somewhere in his house, if you snoop through his drawers while he's in the shower.

Meeting the families of the **Working** group may involve some class or ethnic issues. If you've decided to date that hunky construction worker, be prepared for some differences in tastes and upbringing. These will especially become apparent on home visits. Try to minimize misunderstandings by enthusiastically taking a second helping of the casserole.

Dinner with the family of a **Terrier** may require Valium, since his drive, energy, and argumentative skills were probably acquired at his parents' knees or at their dinner table. Be sure to read the newspaper before you go, and try to remember what you're indignant about today. You may want to think twice before marrying into this family if loud invective bothers you, or if you're not a regular and enthusiastic viewer of CSPAN-2.

The **Toy** may take you home to meet Mummy right away. Be suspicious of this. Does his father seem surprised to meet you? Is your **Toy** boy uncharacteristically demonstrative in front of them? Do his high school art projects still have a prominent place in his mother's house? Did you just discover that he was voted "most likely to star in a Broadway musical" in his high school yearbook? Again, a trip to his house may raise more questions than it answers.

Members of the **Mixed Breed** group often come from loving and supportive nuclear families from someplace in the Midwest. The visit will be uneventful and perhaps even boring. But it's best to sit back and relax, enjoy the bland food and the churchgoing, and hope for a visit from his crazy uncle to liven up the proceedings.

ASK *Elizabeth Taylor*

Dear Elizabeth: I recently visited my boyfriend family's house for the first time, and I was appalled. It's not just that it displayed a complete lack of taste, but it was full of memorabilia from his high school and college days—and he's in his mid-thirties! He had posters of sports cars and pin-ups dating from the Reagan administration, as well as all of his old army men and model toys. I found some heavy-metal tapes that I hope to God he doesn't listen to anymore. Elizabeth, I was truly frightened. What should I do?

Scared in Secaucus

Elizabeth says: This scenario *is* always a little frightening. Remember that boyfriends are creatures of habit, and they prize stability and consistency, especially in their surroundings and habits. Extreme cases of arrested development are sometimes hard to diagnose, because unless the boyfriend is observed in his own habitat, you can write off all the nostalgia for his younger days as cleverly ironic—until the moment when you see that, for real, he's still partying like it's 1989. Fortunately, retraining is possible. You need to wean him off of all his crap and bide your time until, if you end up living together, you can throw it all away.

Dear Elizabeth: I hate my boyfriend's parents—I really do. They are clannish, overprotective, and weird. They only liked one of my boyfriend's previous girlfriends, and that's because she was his cousin. How can I fit in with this tight-knit group, or at least tolerate the yearly holiday dinner?

Outsider in Orlando

Elizabeth says: I hear the strains of banjo music drifting in the background. Are you writing from a cabin in Appalachia? Or a mansion in Newport? (I'm an equal-opportunity critic when it comes to inbreeding.) Some families are so interested in protecting their gene pools and their prize pedigrees that they're willing to put up with a few webbed feet to keep it all in the family. Elizabeth suggests moving as far away from his family as possible and then claiming that the travel time is too long during those busy holiday travel periods. And don't let them get their hands on your kids.

Dear Elizabeth: I feel sorry for my Terrier boyfriend, because he's under a lot of pressure from his parents to go to law school. They're both lawyers, and since birth he's been raised on a steady diet of depositions, writs, and trials. But while he doesn't want to be a lawyer, he's not able to commit to any other profession either. What advice can you give us to help him adjust to a new life?

Illegal in Indio

Elizabeth says: Your boyfriend's problem is that he was bred for a particular task—in this case, lawyering—and has developed special qualities and abilities based on his breed specialization. His parents want him to be a lawyer because it's the easiest way for him to fully realize certain aspects of his personality—his love of argument, his attention to detail, and his ability to think of his day as a series of billable hours. In order for your **Terrier** boyfriend to feel personally fulfilled, he will need to find another profession that requires similar skills. A similar dilemma faces boyfriends from the **Sporting** group who have been forced to adapt to office jobs, which explains the popularity of golf as a means of business socializing.

FOUR

Here, Boy!
The First Few Dates

Once you've chosen which kind of boyfriend you want, it's time to get to know him. The first few dates with a boyfriend set the tone for all of your future interactions, and, because of the importance of strong early bonding in the development of your relationship, careful planning of the first few dates is key.

SOME FIRST-DATE SUGGESTIONS

Below are a number of suggested first dates by type of boyfriend that will promote bonding and maximize its effect.

Sporting
Sporting boyfriends like to stay active, so plan a bike ride, a rock-climbing expedition, or some other outdoor

activity. Wear breathable cotton and be sure to bring along a big picnic.

Hound

Hounds are night crawlers and club goers. Search out an unusual band, concert, or lecture (since **Hounds** consider intellectual stimulation a precursor to other kinds of stimulation). Wear something low cut and bring condoms.

Working

Working boyfriends might like to go to a baseball game or a movie, perhaps a rock concert. They have simple, all-American guy tastes and will be happy with whatever you plan. Wear something cute and bring along a stocked cooler.

Terrier

Terriers will want to do something that you can discuss afterward. Movies, plays, art exhibits, or other cultural events will allow them to display their knowledge to you. Wear something sensible and bring a thesaurus.

Toy

Toys expect the world, so be prepared to give it to them. Make dinner reservations at a fancy restaurant or take him to a movie premiere. It doesn't matter to him what you wear as long as you look fabulous and bring a lot of cash.

Mixed Breed

Mixed Breed boyfriends are amenable to long walks on the beach and picnics at sunset, just like a boyfriend out of a personal ad. Wear something gauzy and leave your cynicism at home.

Bonding Beyond the First Date

"Bonding" is the progressive trust that is built between a woman and her boyfriend. The first three months are the most important: If your boyfriend's experiences with you are positive, your bond will strengthen, and soon he will wag his tail happily whenever he sees you.

"When I met my boyfriend," says Lesley, twenty-seven, "he was still bonded to his former girlfriend,

*the woman I rescued him from. I had to estab-
lish right from the beginning that I was replacing
her, and this meant he wasn't allowed to go to
any of the places he used to go with her. We had
to establish new routines and new favorite spots
so that the memory of her was totally erased
from his mind."*

Kyra's culinary experiences point up the importance of food in establishing a bond: *"I cooked for my boyfriend on the first date—I found out from his friends what his favorite foods were, bought some nice wine, and that was it. He's been eating out of my hand for almost a year now."*

HOW TO BOND WITH YOUR BOYFRIEND

Spend quality time together.

Spending quality time together means committing to rituals and behaviors that you and your boyfriend can look forward to. For example, your boyfriend might enjoy a morning trip to Starbucks or a regular Saturday afternoon drive. He may come to expect the routine, and it's those little things throughout the day that make his life worth living.

Get out in the world and experience life together.
Boyfriends are often happiest when you take them out to meet new people and experience new things. For example, when you take him out for a walk, it will make him happy when beautiful women walk up and start rubbing his belly—just be sure to keep a close eye on him.

Develop a way of communicating so that both of you understand the other's needs.
Once your boyfriend understands clearly when he's doing something right (buying flowers, picking up after himself), and when he's doing something wrong (hogging the bathroom mirror, forgetting to take phone messages), you are *communicating.*

IS THIS AN EFFECTIVE BONDING TOOL?

The options:

1. *Gazing deep into his eyes.*
Y/N

2. Going out together with a big group of your friends.
Y/N

3. Scolding him for being late to meet you.
Y/N

4. Starting to establish a regular time to call him.
Y/N

5. Talking about your ex or his.
Y/N

6. Asking him lots of questions about himself.
Y/N

7. Ignoring his friends when you meet them.
Y/N

8. Finding out his favorite meal and cooking it.
Y/N

9. Telling him a lot about yourself.
Y/N

10. *Getting naked on the first date.*
Y/N

The answers:

1. *Yes!* Gazing deep into his eyes establishes you as the alpha dog. Hold his gaze steadily until he looks away, and repeat as necessary. It can also, incidentally, be romantic.

2. *No!* Going out with a big group of your friends means you cannot do the intensive early work necessary to bond with him. It's too distracting, especially if there are other attractive men or women around. Keep his blinders on!

3. *Yes!* Scolding him for being late to meet you makes him anxious about pleasing you and promotes his feeling that you are someone to be respected. Let him slack off this early, and you'll lose all control.

4. *No!* Starting to establish a regular time to call him is exactly the wrong approach. He should be calling *you* on a regular basis, but it is part of the paradoxical nature of establishing a bond that, while consistency is important, inconsistency has its place. Don't let him grow to expect anything from you on a regular basis at first. This will keep him anxious, on edge, and thinking about you constantly.

5. *No!* Talking about your ex or his is always the wrong choice. Each new relationship is different, and there is nothing to be gained by complaining about the past to each other. And who wants to find out how interesting or cute his last girlfriend was? Your job is to banish the memory of her altogether.

6. *Yes!* Ask him lots of questions about himself. It's important to appear to be interested in him and his needs to let him know you care. Even if your mind wanders during some long technical explanation of his job, you can nod, smile, and say "Mmm hmm" —this attention makes him feel special and bonds him to you.

7. *No!* Ignoring his friends when you meet them is a bad idea. You need to gather as much information as possible about your boyfriend in order to make your retraining of him as easy and fast as possible. Pay attention to the verbal cues dropped by others: "Yes, Spike is always running off like that," and "No, I think Rex finally stopped scratching himself once he stopped wearing those wool pants."

8. *Yes!* Finding out his favorite meal and cooking it is a good way to bond with him. Given how obsessed

with food most boyfriends are, the way to his heart is often still through his stomach. Controlling through food is a good option for women who are not ready to control him through sex.

9. *No!* Telling him a lot about yourself too early in the relationship may damage the sense of mystery and power you need to retain. This isn't about the ticking "Rules" clock that puts time limits on your conversation—this is about the *content* of your conversation. Don't pour your heart out to him too soon. Men are skittish creatures, and you can spook them with sob stories about how not making the cheerleading squad in junior high has scarred you professionally, or how your last boyfriend's refusal to commit now makes you afraid to date. Avoid these boring and disastrous personal revelations and develop actual conversation skills that will impress him with your wit and intelligence. Read a paper and know what's going on in the world. Let your emotional state remain a mystery and hold him in thrall with your mind.

10. *No!* Getting naked on the first date is usually a bad idea. Unless you plan to make this a one-night encounter, save the good stuff for a little later. We're not suggesting you become a thirty-year-old virgin while waiting for the right guy, but keep the upper hand—it's crucial in future training, and bonding works better when you proceed at a slower pace through the early stages of intimacy. Keep him happy and satisfied, but unsatisfied enough to keep coming back. This way, you draw him in slowly— and before you know it, he's totally ensnared in your trap and bonded to you like glue.

Good Boy! Bonding Through Positive Reinforcement

For any subsequent training to be successful, your initial bond must be established and cultivated through positive reinforcement. Be sure to give him lots of positive feed-back and reward him for good behavior.

Boyfriends are also bonded to you through the use of food and physical affection as "treats." Small tidbits of food, or six-packs of beer, may be proffered, as well as frequent petting.

Other treats might include a home-cooked meal (for those hunky **Working** or **Mixed Breed** types who are always hungry), surprise tickets to a baseball game (for those **Sporting** jocks), or going without panties (a surefire way to make those **Hounds** heel). Brainy **Terriers** might enjoy viewing and acting out the scenes from *9½ Weeks*, thereby combining two of their favorite activities, food and sex. **Toy** breeds are especially amenable to this early bonding process: As the lapdogs of the boyfriend world, they like being petted and come to depend on you for all their creature comforts.

As your boyfriend learns to happily accept the food and affection, it is important to make all your experiences with him as pleasant as possible. Don't scold him harshly for any mistakes he makes at this early stage. Only after he begins to show evidence of bonding with you are the more advanced stages of dominance training possible.

ASK
Elizabeth Taylor

Dear Elizabeth: My first date with a Mixed Breed boyfriend was a little dull. How can I turn up the heat next time? He chose the place and the activity (bowling with his parents), and it just didn't go very well.

Disappointed in Duluth

Elizabeth says: You need to take charge here, if you think this is someone you want to see again. Don't worry about an awkward first date—give him another chance to perform well for you. For a **Mixed Breed** boyfriend, you might want to ease him slowly into a more exciting nightlife, one that does not require you to wear someone else's shoes or socialize with his relatives right away. Invite him to your house for dinner, and if you're worried about seeming too "forward," invite some of your friends over as well. A lively night of poker, Scrabble, or Monopoly will allow your **Mixed Breed** man to showcase his modest abilities. Enjoy!

> Dear Elizabeth: How will I be able to tell when my boyfriend is adequately "bonded" to me? What are the signs of that?
>
> Unsure in Yucaipa

Elizabeth says: In the earliest stages of a relationship, when you are just beginning to form a connection with your new boyfriend, you may not see the kind of obedience and devotion you will come to expect from a fully trained boyfriend. In the beginning there might be some recalcitrance on his part to commit to plans or to be at your beck and call. But you can tell the bonding process has begun when he begins to call you more frequently, and when he begins to make long-term plans with you. You will start to feel a strong physical bond with him, and you will miss him when he's not there. Enjoy these early days, because the thrill of a getting to know a new boyfriend and bond with him is one of life's greatest pleasures.

Dear Elizabeth: What have you found to be the most effective way to forge a strong bond with a man? I'm dating a **Working** boyfriend, and I'm having trouble getting through to him emotionally. How do I break down that wall?

Questioning in Quantico

Elizabeth says: Oh, those big, brawny **Working** types can be sweet but hard to get through to. Sometimes, with Larry, I wondered if there *were* deeper emotions to access, but I'm sure that your **Working** man has a vibrant inner life. I met Larry in rehab and I had already been in Group with him, but in the absence of therapy as an ice-breaker, I would suggest taking your **Working** boy to some movies in which people have emotions, or watching television shows displaying emotional content. Afterward, you may be able to discuss the movie and gently turn the conversation toward him. Good luck!

Basic Training
Boot Camp for Boyfriends

To instill the traits that you want your boyfriend to possess—love, loyalty, and an encyclopedic knowledge of your wants and needs—it's necessary to develop some training techniques.

WHAT *IS* TRAINING?

There are three main types of training:

Behavior training teaches your boyfriend to be a "good citizen." This usually includes basic housebreaking, proper "off-leash" manners around other people, and the small behavioral touches that make a boyfriend a pleasant companion. A well-behaved boyfriend attracts no special notice from others, aside from amazing them with his good manners.

Obedience training involves teaching your boyfriend how to perform specific activities on command, such as massage, taking out the trash, and finding your G-spot. The emphasis here is on his prompt and precise performance. Boyfriends that have been obedience-trained will perform specific tasks when their girlfriends ask them to do so.

Activity training refers to training for some specific skills—this might include ballroom dancing, giving the perfect toast, or mixing the perfect cocktail—that will publicly showcase the abilities of a boyfriend and his handler (you).

Tips for Training Your Boyfriend

1. *Start training your boyfriend early on.* While old dogs can be taught new tricks, lessons learned earliest are learned easiest. Get going on that first date: Does he open the door for you? Let you decide which movie to see or which restaurant to eat at? Take control right away.

2. *Train your boyfriend using positive, motivational methods.* Keep obedience sessions fun so it's enjoyable for both of you. You might want to try a "play/training" approach by playing games such as "Go Find Where We Parked the Car and Fetch It."

3. *Whenever possible, use your boyfriend's name positively.* Don't use it only for demands, reprimands, or warnings. Your boyfriend must feel that when he hears his name, good things happen. He should always responds with enthusiasm, not with exasperation or a hasty retreat to his den, where he can be alone.

4. *Catch him before he is about to do something bad.* In training, proper timing is crucial. For example: You've made a beautiful plate of hors d'oeuvres for a cocktail party and left it out. Your boyfriend comes in, sniffs the food, eyes it, and starts to grab a canapé and put it in his mouth. This is the most effective moment to correct your boyfriend: *before* he's misbehaved, while he's only thinking about destroying your array of antipasti.

5. *Don't reinforce his misbehavior by giving him negative attention when he misbehaves.* If your boyfriend gets lots of attention when he forgets to call, for example, his bad behavior is being rewarded, and therefore may be repeated in future bids for attention. Ignore him when he acts up, and he'll come back with his tail between his legs.

6. *Remember, you have something he wants.* Experts are divided on the efficacy of early introduction of "physical affection" as a bonding tool. Small, measured doses of affection tend to keep your new boyfriend adequately bonded to you, but if a long-term relationship is not your goal, more affection is fine. In order for you to maintain the dominant position in a long-term relationship, you must control the timing and amount of physical affection and keep him panting for more. (For more on sex and your boyfriend, see Chapter 7, "Get Off My Leg!")

Which Type of Training Is Right for My Boyfriend?

If your boyfriend is the strong, take-charge type (**Sporting, Working,** some **Terriers**), a method that does not take this trait into account will result in his dominating you during the training sessions. Conversely, if your boyfriend is very sensitive (some **Toys** and **Terriers,** some **Hounds** and **Mixed Breeds**), there may be a variety of methods you can use so long as you are very careful about how you correct him. A submissive boyfriend may require training that emphasizes learning new things very thoroughly so that they are as confident as possible when performing new tasks.

PAVLOV, MEET SKINNER: TWO SCHOOLS OF TRAINING

Classical "Pavlovian" conditioning

The principles of classical conditioning were worked out early in this century by Pavlov. A bell was rung, and the subject (it was a dog, but you can easily imagine your boyfriend) was given food. The dog began to salivate on hearing the bell, anticipating the arrival of the food.

How can Pavlovian conditioning be applied to boyfriend training?

You train your boyfriend by voicing a command ("Buy me a present"), and then treating him with a primary reward (say, sex). He'll begin to associate the two and will respond to the command whether or not a reward is actually proffered.

Skinnerian "operant conditioning"

B. F. Skinner outlined the principles of operant conditioning, in which the reinforcement cycle starts with some action on the part of the boyfriend/trainee. It is *always* dependent on behavior: Your boyfriend does something (buys a gift, or forgets to) and then gets positive reinforcement (sex) or punishment (no sex).

How can Skinnerian training be used to train my boyfriend?

By controlling which behaviors are reinforced (here, gift giving), you get the boyfriend to behave that way more often. If he gets rewards in association with a particular behavior, he's likely to repeat it; if something bad happens, he's less likely to repeat it.

Combining elements of both

A combined sequence would look like this, and it's fun for both of you:

1. Boyfriend does something good (buys a gift).
2. Boyfriend is rewarded (with, say, sex).
3. Cycle continues until boyfriend continually offers gifts.
4. You now say, "Buy more expensive gifts."
5. He does.
6. He is rewarded (with more sex).

Rewards and Punishments: How to Use Them

Rewards should be given in such a way as to increase the incidence of desirable behavior, and they should be something your boyfriend enjoys and is motivated by. A few boyfriends seem to be motivated by verbal praise, though not to the degree you would like to think. Boyfriends learn to accept verbal praise ("Good boy") only as a secondary reward through association with a desirable *primary* reward (a treat). With a few exceptions, almost every boyfriend views food and/or sex as a treat, and modifies his behavior accordingly. Conversely, punishment should involve the withholding of rewards or affection, along with certain physical checks or curbs.

REWARDS AND PUNISHMENTS, BY BOYFRIEND GROUP

Hound

Reward: You wear crotchless panties while training him.

Punishment: Emptying out the bottle of good vodka.

Terrier

Reward: You agree to read the draft of his op-ed letter to the *Times*.

Punishment: Hiding his *Wall Street Journal*.

Toy

Reward: A trip to the salon for a pedicure (his and hers).

Punishment: Polyester sheets on the bed.

Working

Reward: A six-pack and a blow job.

Punishment: Forced to watch made-for-Lifetime movies with you.

Sporting

Reward: A shiny new ball.

Punishment: Instead of golfing on a sunny weekend, you both visit your mother.

Mixed Breed

Reward: A kiss and a smile.

Punishment: None of your special casserole for dinner this week!

Top Five Boyfriend Training Videos

1. *How to Teach Your Boyfriend to Get Used to the Collar and Leash*

2. *Your Boyfriend, Your Boundaries*

3. *How to Train Your Boyfriend to Listen*

4. *How to Teach Your Boyfriend to Call*

5. *How to Teach Your Boyfriend to Come, Every Time You Call*

ASK
Elizabeth Taylor

Dear Elizabeth: My boyfriend has terrible manners. He never holds doors or allows me to go first. He's quite rude! I've tried to get him to act like a gentleman by bringing up his bad habits many times, but I'm losing patience. How do I get his attention? I'm thinking about using more forceful techniques, such as a shock collar or a big whip, to get my point across. What do you suggest?

Mad in Manhattan

Elizabeth says: Save the whips and collars for another time, because after-the-fact discipline is not effective. You need to make your needs known to your boyfriend *before* he makes the mistake again. Teaching and communication is what it's all about, not punishing your boyfriend. If you're taking an "it's-you-against-him, whip-him-into-shape" approach, you'll undermine your relationship, while missing out on all the fun that a motivational training approach can offer . . . although Elizabeth thinks that light bondage can be fun, and might be considered motivational by some.

Dear Elizabeth: I just can't bring myself to punish my boyfriend when he's been bad. I look into those big brown eyes of his and I just melt, no matter how angry I am. Help! I know I'm creating a monster, but I can't stop myself!

Weak-willed in Wichita

Elizabeth says: Girls, girls, girls, you *must* learn to be a strong-willed mistress! Noone wants to have an untrained boyfriend piddling all over the toilet seat and leaving his socks around the house. *No matter how cute he is,* he will be *much* cuter with good manners. So, if you consistently reward your boyfriend with love and affection despite his bad behavior, or if you fail to punish him, two things happen: First, his behavior will never improve because he has no feedback about what is acceptable, and, second, he learns that he always get rewarded, so his incentive to behave will decrease or disappear. Eventually, your affection will no longer be seen as a reward but an entitlement, and you will no longer have any control over his behavior whatsoever. Elizabeth shudders to think of such a situation.

SIX

Why Won't My Boyfriend Listen to Me?

Establishing Communication Right from the Start

"Training" and "communication" are virtually synonymous. Being able to communicate with your boyfriend allows you to go anywhere and do anything with him, knowing that that he'll listen and obey you. But it is not always clear how much your boyfriend understands or whether he is actually even listening to you.

When he first comes home with you, it is as if he has been sent to you from a foreign country, so he must be shown what you mean by particular words and phrases ("Fetch me a skim latte," "Please pick up that wet towel").

Many women complain that their boyfriends are "stubborn" and that they "refuse to listen" when given a command. You need to figure out if your boyfriend knows what you want and knows how to comply, or if he is not responding because of fear, confusion, or the fact that he's watching the playoffs and doesn't hear you at all.

Hear, Boy!

Here are some important tips for communicating effectively with your boyfriend:

When giving your boyfriend a command, avoid using a loud voice.

Even if he is independent or unresponsive, your tone of voice when issuing an obedience command such as "Fetch the groceries out of the car," "Stop changing the channels on the TV," or "Pick up that trash and take it out" should not be angry, but calm.

Master a commanding tone.

You need not speak softly all the time, yet you also do not need to yell or whine at him. Women have an easy time with the "Good Boyfriend" tone of voice, one that is high-pitched, soft, and sweet. But they need to master the "Bad Boyfriend" tone and the "Command" tone, since boyfriends often pay attention to tone of voice and not to the content of the sentence at all.

You're not asking him to do something, you're telling him.

Many women have particular trouble getting boyfriends to obey the "Command" tone of voice, most often because their sentence sounds more like a question, with their voice raising at the end of the command. Shake the Valley Girl accent and keep your commands firm, short, and sweet.

Using Body Language to Break Through to Him

Boyfriends operate instinctually. Even when they are not listening to what you are saying, they are absorbing cues from your behavior about the content of your speech. Here are nonverbal ways to make your discussions with him more effective.

1. *Body language:* Boyfriends are often staring at your breasts. Invest in message T-shirts.

2. *Vocal intonation and voice inflection:* Don't get too high-pitched—it's only a myth that they can hear those upper registers. Those are the ones they've specifically learned not to hear.

3. *Touch:* Patting his head, stroking his hand, or massaging other parts of his body hinders serious discussion. Use this only as a last resort, when you need to get a "yes" out of him when he's distracted.

4. *Scent:* The aroma of food will create positive associations with what you are saying in his mind. Stand in front of him with a steak when you're asking him about "where you are" in the relationship.

Oh, Behave!
How to Communicate with Him

Once you've mastered how to say it, you need to know what to say. Men always complain they don't understand women, so the chart below makes it simple for you to break down the elements of the major commands for him in an easy-to-understand manner.

SIT!	The most basic command, the one on which his other obedience skills are built.	If you can train him in the "sit/stay" (see below), you have established yourself as the alpha dog. Controlling his urge to roam is essential.

STAY!	Works on restless or bored boyfriends in many different situations.	You don't want him wandering off while you are shopping, or leaving the bar to follow some other girl, so you use the "stay" command to keep him in his place.
COME!	Double-entendres aside, a useful command for the errant boyfriend.	If he's been roaming far and wide lately, you need to get him to return to you, promptly and without excuse. He should respond with alacrity to your phone call or page.
HEEL!	Well-behaved boyfriends excel at the "heel" command, in which they are present at your side, alert, and attentive.	This is most often used at parties and other social occasions, where your boyfriend is there with a fresh drink for you or carrying your bag.

FETCH!	One of the great all-purpose commands.	Cars, jewelry, flowers, dinner, what *cannot* be fetched? A well-trained boyfriend will respond to this command by fetching you the *proper* form of the item you asked for.
ROLL OVER!	What he does when you win the argument.	You are right, and he needs to respect and acknowledge that when he "rolls over."
BEG!	You have to make him.	Boyfriends want what they can't have, so begging is the manifestation of the important psychological advantage you hold over him.

DOWN!	For boyfriends who jump too much.	If he's always on your leg, this is the command that will get him off it. Also works when he pesters guests.
GET OFF!	Sometimes he comes in too dirty to get near the furniture.	If he's about to put his muddy paws on the white sofa, this command works quickly and effectively.
SHAKE!	You can teach him to greet others politely.	This is the best party trick for your boyfriend: He can impress your friends with his politeness and good breeding.
SPEAK!	You can make him communicate.	The problem is making him say the things you actually want to hear, like what's he feeling.

"Miss Communication"
Making Yourself Understood, Part One

On those rare occasions when he is listening to you, there can still be problems. One of the biggest relationship pitfalls is misunderstanding and miscommunication. Some common "translation" errors, explained:

What you say	*What he hears*
"Will you call me next week?"	"I love you madly and want to marry you—next week."
"I have two tickets to the ballet."	"I think you're gay."
"I have two tickets to the Knicks."	"I want to sleep with you."
"We need to talk."	"I have decided to have a long, boring, one-sided conversation about 'us.'"
"You never listen to me."	" ."
"Does this make me look fat?"	"I am deciding whether to throw up lunch or not."
"Do you think she is cute?"	"Maybe we could have a three-way with her."

What you say	*What he hears*
"Do you think he is cute?"	"I will never, ever have sex with you. Forget about it."
"No, don't worry about it, I understand."	"I have already posted the personal ad for your replacement."
"Oh, he's just a friend."	"We are having sex at my office in the supply closet."
"Sure, my friends like you."	"We're considering a three-way with you."
"My parents liked you a lot."	"I love you madly and want to marry you—next week."
"I've never had it this good before."	"I've never had it this good before, you big stud."
"Of course size doesn't matter!"	"I have already posted the personal ad for your replacement."
"Hi."	"I want to sleep with you."

"Miss Communication" Making Yourself Understood, Part Two

The following is a list you can give him that will provide the actual meaning of the statements above. This will help him understand what you mean, every time.

What you say	*What you mean*
"Will you call me next week?"	"I cannot understand how men view the passage of time—are you ever planning to call me?"
"I have two tickets to the ballet."	"I'm trying to see just how much you like me."
"I have two tickets to the Knicks."	"You're cute, so I spent a lot of money to lure you on a date."
"We need to talk."	"My girlfriends have brought some more of your personal flaws to my attention."
"You never listen to me."	"I know very well that you are not listening to me at this very moment."
"Does this make me look fat?"	"If you answer this the wrong way, you will never see me naked again."
"Do you think she is cute?"	"Is she cuter than I am?"
"Do you think he is cute?"	"I just found your disco collection, and I'm a little worried."
"No, don't worry about it, I understand."	"You have one more chance."
"Oh, he's just a friend."	"He'd be your replacement, so you better behave."
"Sure, my friends like you."	"They are looking for someone new to set me up with."

What you say	What you mean
"My parents liked you a lot."	"They are relieved you have no criminal convictions like my last boyfriend did."
"I've never had it this good before."	"Where did I put my vibrator?"
"Of course size doesn't matter!"	"Did I remember to cross my fingers when I said that?"
"Hi."	"Your friend is cute and I'm too shy to talk to him."

ASK
Elizabeth Taylor

Dear Elizabeth: My boyfriend and I seem to be having trouble coming to an agreement on what certain things mean. For example, when I ask him to clean up the kitchen after we eat, I expect to find the kitchen cleaned, but he just usually throws everything away, including the dishes and the silverware. And when I give him instructions in bed, he seems to be having some trouble following them. Help!

Misunderstood in Memphis

Elizabeth says: Oops! It's true that men and women often speak different languages, but there are other reasons for communication problems. Men hear "clean the kitchen" and they just shut down emotionally. They may be fearful of engaging in housework, and you need to show them carefully how to complete their chores from start to finish. In bed, it's a similar matter. Many men cannot find your G-spot without a lighted miner's helmet and a map, so provide them with the tools they need to get the job done. It's all about defining the terms and explaining the territory up front.

SEVEN

"Get Off My Leg!"
Sex and Your Boyfriend

The "Reward" of Physical Affection

The most powerful motivational tools in boyfriend training are sex and affection. You possess what your boyfriend
most wants in life, besides food or courtside seats, and the
judicious use of your sexual power is the basis of all successful training.

Keep this one fact in mind: Boyfriends want what
they cannot have. In order to establish yourself as the
alpha dog in the relationship, remember the following
paradox: You need to be both predictable in rewarding
him and yet sometimes remain unpredictable. If your
boyfriend is sometimes unsure whether he will receive a

treat, he will remain anxious, on-edge, and obedient. He never knows when you might bestow something good on him. Keep the upper hand at all times.

To Pet, or Not to Pet?

If you desire a long-term boyfriend, the odds are usually better if you keep him on a short leash and restrict his activities for the first few dates. Everyone has heard of that couple who met and went straight for the heavy, heavy petting on the first date, but those stories are out-numbered by the experiences of the many women who find themselves without the leverage provided by sex if they let their boyfriend "off the leash" too early.

FROM "SHAKE!" TO EARTHSHAKING: THE SEX SPECTRUM

On the leash

While he's still being kept "on the leash," you both stick to anything that can properly be done at a cocktail party or in front of a maiden aunt. Nuzzling, nipping, notongue kissing, and hand-holding get him all hot and bothered and wanting more. Think of Cary Grant or Fred Astaire, and imagine that you're in a black-and-white '40s movie. It's the most dizzyingly romantic and fun phase of any relationship—one you will look back on fondly and try to re-create on anniversaries and special occasions.

Cuddling

This is a concept you may need to introduce with charts and illustrations. Your boyfriend is usually not hard-wired to consider this a part of his sexual repertoire, but like any creature he may quickly discover the joys of just curling up happily with you.

Light petting

Also known as the second date, or second base, light petting involves French kissing and semi-chaste over-the-clothes contact, the kind that can happen on your front step or in the car as you're saying good night. You'll feel like you're in high school again, when obstacles like your parents made all sexual contact more exciting. Years into your relationship, when you and your bored husband have sex in the backseat of your family-friendly minivan, you'll be doing it to recapture the thrill of these early days.

Check out classic high-school movies like *Pretty in Pink* to get some pointers about how hot this stage can be.

Heavy petting

This is the kind of "A" that should not be part of PDA unless you are a call girl. It includes below-the-neck activity as well as titillating states of undress. It's hard to have too many petting sessions without going "all the way" fairly quickly. It's usually during these moments that the "sofa-or-the bed" conversation happens, and only you can decide how "comfortable" you want your boyfriend to be. It's a good idea to keep these extended petting sessions short, in order to keep him in thrall to you for as long as possible.

The Full Monica

This is, honestly, one of the major training tools in your arsenal, used as a reward or withheld as a punishment. Skill and talent in this area can bring great changes in your boyfriend's behavior, from picking up his socks to picking up presents from Tiffany's. And no one has done more to raise the profile and promote the public acceptance of oral sex than Monica Lewinsky and her **Hound** boyfriend, Bill. Older people were shocked to discover that, in post–*Deep Throat* America, many under the age of fifty concurred with Bill's contention that this "wasn't sex." And while it's the appetizer of choice for most men, make sure of two things: It can never become his main course and turnabout is fair play.

Off the leash

What can you say about this one? Allowing your boyfriend (or, if you reside in the Bible Belt, your husband) full off-leash privileges is a mark of trust, both in his future fidelity and in the obedience skills you've been working on during your petting sessions together. When you say "there" or "more" he should know exactly what you mean and do it right away.

ROMANCE AND SEX TIPS FOR DIFFERENT BOYFRIEND BREEDS

Once you are weeks or months into the relationship, and romping happily with your new boyfriend, it's important to know how to keep his tail wagging. Some type-specific tips:

Working boyfriends are basic, bread-and-butter guys: "*Kama* what?" They won't want any fancy positions, but they'll want lots of it. Subtle or complicated lingerie is lost on them and might be damaged. He's a traditionalist, so no lights and no trying anything weird.

Get in shape for your sessions with a **Sporting** boyfriend. He prizes athleticism, flexibility, and a certain amount of imagination, along with firm abs. Remember to do some sit-ups. Again, stay away from the kinky stuff, but be prepared for him to display his prowess between the sheets, since he never loses that competitive spirit of his.

The Marquis de Sade was a **Hound,** so prepare for a wild ride. Give a jolt to his jaded appetites by wearing white cotton panties—it will be a new thrill for him. He's seen it all and done it all, most likely, but you will be the satisfied beneficiary of his vast experience. Make it clear up front what you're not willing to do.

There will be an earnest, learned quality to your **Terrier's** endeavors to please you (because he will have read up on the subject and be ready to, ahem, apply his newly acquired knowledge). But their dogged persistence and desire to please make these boyfriends some of the most reliable sources of real pleasure.

Depending on the exact leanings of your **Toy** boy, sex may or may not be part of this relationship. If he's in denial about his **Toy** status, you may be in for some awkward fumbling and ultimate frustration. But if he's one of those **Toys** who only *seems* like a **Toy,** he will most likely be a rather selfish sex partner, since, with his good looks, he's used to being catered to. But he's so cute, who wouldn't want to cuddle with him?

The pleasures of plain-vanilla sex with a handsome, balanced **Mixed Breed** boyfriend should not be under-estimated. This is the partner of choice for many women without the physical stamina to keep up with the **Working** or **Sporting** boyfriends or the patience to put up with the selfishness of the **Toys,** and who have out-grown the kinkiness of the diabolical **Hounds.**

CASE STUDY

WALLIS SIMPSON, DUCHESS OF WINDSOR AND . . . SEXPOT?

American divorcée Wallis Simpson brought her charms to bear on England's Edward VIII, who abdicated the throne of England rather than live without the "help and support of the woman I love." Simpson, a well-known dog lover undoubtedly familiar with the principles of obedience training, was also rumored to have honed her bedroom skills in a Chinese brothel prior to enthralling the weak-willed king. (Given Wallis and Edward's unfortunate sympathy for Hitler and his Nazi party, it can be argued that her talents in the boudoir were beneficial for England, which might be a German province today if the Duchess hadn't been so . . . skilled.) Immediate benefits for the Duchess herself included the devoted lifetime services of her new lapdog, Edward, and all the jewelry she could wear.

How to Keep Him on the Porch

If your boyfriend has a wandering eye (a common afflic-
tion of the **Hound** group), here are some tips for making
sure you remain his sole mistress. Men are weak creatures,
and you can only trust their higher instincts so far—at
some point, their baser instincts are likely to prevail.

1. *Keep him busy.*
A busy boyfriend is a boyfriend who doesn't have the
time for wandering eyes. If you're at a party, make sure
that he has plenty to do: holding your drinks, fetching
your drinks, holding your bag or coat, fetching your bag
or coat . . . you get the idea.

2. *Limit his opportunities.*
Hillary's first mistake was to leave Bill alone with other
women without hiding in a nearby closet holding the
controls to his shock collar. But in less extreme situations,
you should assess the situations your boyfriend might find
himself in (at work, at the gym, etc.), and evaluate whether
his loyalty and obedience will be tested beyond its limits.

3. *Know his pack.*

Your boyfriend's friends are a potent influence on him. Pack behavior explains such tacky or otherwise inexplicable phenomena as Hooters, fraternity hazing, and the entire *Girls Gone Wild* video series. Packs create situations in which the lowest common denominator will always prevail. Consider getting him new friends, perhaps neutered ones or **Toy** ones. Maybe an all-male knitting club?

4. *Retrain him.*

It's possible to work to change your boyfriend's inborn instinct to stray. Remember, he is evolutionarily programmed to try to share his genetic material with as many women as possible, so don't become angry with him when he blindly attempts to follow that natural directive. Instead, reinforce the fact that he is not an animal who needs to hump every leg in sight.

5. *Keep him happy at home.*

A happy and sexually contented boyfriend stays on the porch, and you get to have fun, too! If you're not willing to make him happy in this way, you might want to question why you're clinging to him so jealously. By building a solid relationship based on trust and hot sex, you'll be able to take him out in any situation and know that he won't stray from your side.

106
Troubleshooting Tip #106

The problem: My boyfriend is "excited" all the time— jumping, licking, humping the furniture, and really wearing me out, if you know what I mean.

Why he does this: Exuberance and a high sex drive is normal in younger boyfriends, but if he's not a teenager, his constant excitement is unnatural (although not unwelcome to some women; if it really bothers you, you might consider giving him away to someone who appreciates his "energy"). Maybe he is not getting enough exercise, or perhaps he spends too much time alone and is starved for attention by the time he sees you.

What to do: Spend twenty minutes of "quiet time" with him that does not involve sex. Pet him quietly, maybe give him a massage. Train him so that he learns to control himself when he is around you, and make sure he gets plenty of exercise so that he's worn out by the time you get home. Make sure also that he has other things to do that hold his interest—plenty of toys, distractions, and hobbies, like Internet porn. If he still gets too wild for you, apply a quick physical correction such as a light slap or pinch and tell him, "Off!"

Why this is effective: In getting adequate exercise and finding other distractions, and by engaging in quiet time with you, your boyfriend will become mellower and more contented.

How to prevent this: Make sure that his needs are met, even if it means you give him permission to meet them "alone."

Troubleshooting Tip #767

The problem: Whenever my boyfriend sees another woman, he makes a move on her, and if he's off-leash, he chases her.

Why he does this: Chasing other women is instinctual in

most boyfriends, who are almost all descended from hunters and still find a thrill in the chase.

What to do: It can be difficult to get your boyfriend to stop such an instinctual behavior, but through mastering some obedience commands—especially "heel"—you can control him when you are out with him. Take him out for a walk and keep him at your side. The instant your boyfriend sees another woman (his ears will perk up excitedly), tighten your grip on his arm just as he is about to move toward her. If he calms down, praise him: "Good boy. Good to leave the pretty lady alone." Reward him with more praise and some publicly acceptable physical affection.

Why this is effective: Anticipating when your boyfriend is thinking about chasing another woman (and correcting him immediately) is more effective than correcting him after he's started to make his move.

How to prevent this: Never encourage your boyfriend to assess other women ("Do you think she's pretty?") and limit his unsupervised socializing with them. Make sure he gets plenty of affection from you so that he won't seek it from others.

EIGHT

Housebreaking 101
Bringing Home a New Boyfriend

As your relationship progresses, you will begin spending time with your new boyfriend at your house. His house will still be uninhabitable, since it's not yet been renovated, redecorated, or made passably habitable by you.

Introducing him into your home environment furthers his socialization process. Socialization is the process of conforming to group living and adjusting and adapting to the needs of a social group. Many boyfriends have difficulties understanding the needs of the "group's" alpha dog (i.e., you), and may need specific training to help them adapt to their new environment.

Toys, Terriers, and **Mixed Breed** boyfriends are often good around the house: **Toys** because they like to help rearrange the furniture, **Terriers** because of their compulsive drive to organize, and **Mixed Breed**

boyfriends because they are so naturally sweet and pli-able. **Working, Sporting,** and **Hound** boyfriends are less well-adapted to home life: **Working** because they're often too big and a little too clumsy to be trusted with glassware, **Sporting** because it's impossible to drag them away from the game to help cook, and **Hounds** because they usually slink out early the morning after and you never see them again.

Banishing Previous Bad Training

Before you got your boyfriend, he may have been social-ized in different environments. When you are able to isolate one of them and bring them into civilized captiv-ity, it is important to introduce them slowly to manners and grooming. Some boyfriends may have forgotten how to use silverware or china (pizza can be eaten with your fingers on paper plates), how to put the lid of the toilet down (why would you need to do that?), or how to change the sheets on their bed with any regularity (huh?). Here are possible living histories:

Used to live with his parents

While he may not need to adjust to life with other people, he may still expect his mother-substitute to do his laundry and clean up after him. You will need to recondition this kind of boyfriend by introducing him to the use of the washing machine and the dishwasher. In Italy, for example, Italian men never move away from their mother because they can never get someone to take care of them like their mamas do. These men are often spoiled, and moving in with you may be a shock to their systems.

Used to live in a pack with other men

If he is young, your boyfriend may have lived in a single-sex environment, and may therefore have returned to a feral state, one in which his natural instincts will have taken over. Feral boyfriends scavenge food in packs, drink large quantities of alcohol, and dispense with hygiene altogether. (Most **Working** and **Sporting** boyfriends have lived this way.)

Used to live alone

Older boyfriends may have lived by themselves. They may be completely or partially socialized, but perhaps not to your standards or specifications (See "The Half-

Trained Boyfriend" case study on page 123.) Boyfriends who lived alone may also be creatures of habit, set in their ways and unaccustomed to the kind of obedience work that you will require of them.

Used to live with a different girlfriend

You may expect a boyfriend who is trained if you get a boyfriend who has already lived with someone else. But she may have had different expectations, or he may be scarred from too-vigorous training, or he may be one of the untrainable boyfriends whom no woman is capable of subduing. You might want to make discreet inquiries about his habits before taking him on, to see which category he belongs to.

Set Clear Expectations

In order to maintain your alpha status, it's important for you to set rules for your boyfriend to follow.

Do

Wait until he is acknowledged to speak or approach.

Kiss but do not slobber.

Know which pieces of furniture he is allowed on.

Use good manners when eating.

Be polite in public and private.

Rein in his sex drive and wait till the appropriate time to express it.

Don't

Demand attention.

Perform unnecessary licking, slobbering, nipping, or mouthing.

Jump up onto the bed without permission.

Hoard food.

Beg.

Growl.

Behave aggressively.

Fight with other boyfriends.

Hump the furniture.

"Pet Peeves": Real Women Speak Up

Leaving clothes on the floor, especially socks

"Shedding" everywhere and leaving hair in the drain

Bad "bathroom habits," including not putting the seat down, not aiming, getting *everything* in the bathroom wet, not rinsing out the sink or the shower

Using all their girlfriend's products—we can smell them on you!

Bad "kitchen habits," including leaving food to rot in the refrigerator, eating out of jars with fingers, drinking out of shared cartons, leaving crumbs everywhere, leaving food out

Bad "bedroom habits," including unrestrained flatulence, coffee breath, hogging the covers, snoring and denying it, and hogging the whole bed and all the pillows

Bad "living room habits," including relentless channel surfing, watching TV all day long, sleeping on the couch and ignoring chores, leaving the newspaper everywhere, and hogging the newspaper

CASE STUDY

THE "HALF-TRAINED" BOYFRIEND

Some boyfriends have been partially trained, either by their mothers or by previous girlfriends. A half-trained boyfriend possesses many of the attributes that you want him to have: He may know where the washing machine is, or the dishwasher, or even the vacuum. The tragedy of the half-trained boyfriend, however, is that he will embark on a chore but be unable to complete it. For example, he will load the dishwasher, but forget to turn it on, or he will leave half-dry clothing in the dryer for several days, resulting in mildewed clothing.

Don't get too angry at the half-trained boyfriend, because you can recognize that he is trying. Use positive reinforcement to commend him for the part of the task that he has completed, and work to encourage him to complete the task—running and emptying the dishwasher, washing and folding the clothes, or taking the garbage all the way out to the curb.

Troubleshooting Tip #867

Problem: My boyfriend escapes from our yard on the weekends and runs aimlessly around the neighborhood. I'm afraid he might get lost or hit by a car.

Why he does this: First, be sure what he's doing isn't jogging. If it's not some form of legitimate exercise, your boyfriend is probably bored with his activities in your home and wants to see what else is out there.

What to do: If you catch him pawing at the fence, shoo him away while firmly saying "No!" If he insists on escaping, wait outside and catch him in the act, and shame him into going back into the house to help you with the weekend chores.

Why this is effective: Catching your boyfriend in the act of escaping and humiliating him into returning to the yard is effective and is a more humane alternative than physical restraints or an electric fence.

How to prevent this: Create a good quality life for your boyfriend at home: Make sure he does not spend his whole weekend stuck at home doing boring chores.

Give him lots of attention and take him out with you often enough that he won't feel the need to bolt on the weekends.

Troubleshooting Tip #5309

The problem: When my boyfriend wants my attention, he makes loud noises and whines. This is a problem, especially when I am busy or on the telephone.

Why he does this: He wants some of the attention you are giving the telephone or your other activities, and he knows that if he makes noise you will acknowledge him in some way.

What to do: As soon as he makes noise, use a physical correction like a small slap and tell him, "Quiet! No whining!"

Why this is effective: By reacting quickly, you are able to correct him as soon as he starts making noise.

How to prevent this: Make sure he gets some quality time with you every day. Provide him with toys and treats beforehand so he has something to distract him while you are busy doing something else. Don't reward his bad behavior with treats to distract him after the fact—this will only reinforce the behavior.

Troubleshooting Tip #666

The problem: My boyfriend acts afraid of everyday household items like the vacuum, the dishwasher, and the washing machine.

Why he does this: Objects that are unfamiliar to him, or that make loud noises, or that are involved in household chores may spook him. He may associate these objects with "women's work" or other frightening things.

What to do: Try to work with your boyfriend near the scary object, but stay far enough away so that he is not spooked. As he gains confidence, slowly move closer to the object, praising him constantly. As he becomes more relaxed, start to turn on the various objects when he is near them, and you two can discuss what they do. For example, slowly open the lid of the washer and talk reassuringly to him as you separate whites from darks and load the machine. Gradually work up to the point where he is not only unafraid of the machine, but is willing to get close enough to use it himself.

Why this is effective: This slow approach works step-by-step to allow your boyfriend to acquaint himself with various frightening objects, and training him in their use will increase his confidence and reduce his fears.

How to prevent this: Never use household objects to tease or frighten your boyfriend. If he shies away from them, speak soothingly and encourage him to investigate them at his own pace.

Troubleshooting Tip #1010

The problem: My boyfriend is sometimes unnecessarily possessive: He gets hold of an object, like the remote control to the television, and refuses to relinquish it. He sometimes even snaps at me when I try to take it away from him.

Why he does this: Your boyfriend, like all men, is attracted to gadgets and is sentimentally attached to the toys he feels are "his." When he gets upset when they are taken away, it may be because he feels entitled to the object and because he does not respect you as his pack leader.

What to do: The most effective way to release his grip on an object is to offer him a trade—offer him another of his toys or food or sex in exchange for dropping it. You should also work on establishing yourself more clearly as the one in control if you are having trouble getting him to obey you.

Why this is effective: By trading with him, you will ensure that your boyfriend won't feel deprived of the object, and he will usually comply with your requests.

How to prevent this: Don't be angry when trying to pry something out of his paws. Instead, provide him with enough toys that he will be willing to drop what he has.

Troubleshooting Tip #967

The problem: Whenever my boyfriend sees anyone eating, he drools greedily and stares at the refrigerator or the plate the person is eating off of.

Why he does this: Your boyfriend, like most men, is a little piggy when it comes to food.

What to do: If he starts bothering you or others for food, tell him "No begging!" in an annoyed voice, disgustedly shoo him away, and say "Go away!" If he continues to beg or look at you beseechingly, send him out of the room.

Why this is effective: By being assertive with him, you establish yourself as the "alpha dog," and this position gives you the right to keep him away from your food.

How to prevent this: Always feed your boyfriend his meals and snacks on his own plate, and don't let him eat off of your plate. Make sure he's eating a healthy diet, so that you're sure his begging is just greediness and not health-related.

SOME TIPS FOR BOYFRIEND-PROOFING YOUR HOME

Is your house ready for a boyfriend? Before bringing him over or leaving him there alone for any period of time, be sure to consider the following things:

Make sure that all embarrassing or incriminating materials of yours are hidden away.

Bored boyfriends who are left unattended might rifle through the trash and find something you don't want them to.

Coasters, coasters, coasters.

A new boyfriend, while cute, can be very destructive. Be sure to have coasters and napkins ready so that he doesn't resort to wiping his fingers on your sofa cushions.

Train him to keep his paws off your stuff!

Be sure he knows which towels are his and that he is not allowed to use your razor, toothbrush, shampoo, or other grooming products, unless you specify that he can. Ditto for any toys he finds in the apartment: Be clear about what he can chew on and what he must drop immediately.

A recently fed boyfriend is a happy boyfriend.

In the kitchen, it's a good idea to stock the fridge with some treats that can be used for positive reinforcement during training. Heineken and smoked meats and cheeses are a good bet.

Set boundaries for him.

You may want to keep part or parts of your apartment cordoned off as a "no-boyfriend" zone. This might include particularly delicate or easily stained furniture, or it might be the small room or closet where you stash everything you don't want him to ruin, find, or see. A small gate or a large lock is usually suitable.

NINE

Sit Up, Boy!
Exercising, Feeding, and Grooming Your Boyfriend

With the exception of **Toy** boys, who might have a thing or two to teach *you* about grooming and personal care, most women find it necessary to intervene in this aspect of their boyfriends' lives.

He's Naked Under There: Body Basics

Your boyfriend's bright eyes and good looks begin with the good health that comes from eating right and exercising. Help him stay on a regular program of sleeping, eating, and exercising by joining him in all three. The couple that lifts weights together will never have those flabby upper arms that jiggle.

TYPES OF EXERCISE, BY BREED

Keeping your boyfriend fit, trim, and healthy is important for his looks and his mood. Here are some tips, by boyfriend group.

Sporting boyfriends may prefer team sports and other activities that allow them to show off. On a daily basis, he will be begging to go to the gym or run outside, so don't stand in his way—let him get all the exercise his type needs.

Working boyfriends may have a strenuous job, so you should take that into account. On the weekends, encourage him to get off the couch and join you for a little bowling or perhaps a little soccer with his friends.

Terriers burn a lot of energy just being themselves. Keep him fit and alert by letting him a chase a little black ball or a big yellow one—squash and tennis are right for his type.

Hounds were bred for the chase, but not for "exercise." Keep him indoors with some between-the-sheets play—it's the only team sport these boyfriends like to participate in.

Toys have a lot of energy, but may find certain kinds of exercise sweaty and distasteful. Yoga, swimming, skiing— these are the kinds of exercise **Toys** prefer.

Mixed Breed boyfriends, like **Sporting** boyfriends, are amenable to and good at many different types of sports, from golf to the corporate softball team to soccer, tennis, or skiing.

He's Not a Puppy Anymore

As your boyfriend moves through his twenties and thirties, changes take place, and you will have to help him adjust his feeding and grooming routines and modify his behavior accordingly.

Terrible Twenties: He's still got that puppyish energy and exuberance, and this may be manifest in excessive partying and staying out late. Make sure he eats regular, healthy meals and doesn't drink too much or take too many drugs. As he gets through his twenties he will start to settle down and be more compliant. You should work on moving him away from his casual wardrobe into a more adult mode of dressing.

Dirty Thirties: He will become more willful and set in his ways, and you need to make sure that he eats right and exercises to keep him trim. He will usually start to

slow down on the partying; men who don't are usually
headed for AA. Watch him carefully. Sexually, he will be
getting better and more skilled, if a little less energetic,
and his clothing sense may still need some fine tuning.
Fascinating Forties and Beyond: If your boyfriend is
this old and has never married, he may be a permanent
"boyfriend"—i.e., stuck in the Peter Pan mode forever.
Approach with caution. Divorced older men will usually
be better trained and know how to care for themselves
in regards to grooming and exercise but may need some
fashion pointers, as their sense of what's fashionable may
date from the '70s or '80s. If your boyfriend is in his
fifties or beyond, consult medical journals and keep an
oxygen tank handy.

WHAT SHOULD I FEED MY BOYFRIEND, AND WHY?

A Quick Quiz

The questions:

1. *Boyfriends do best when you make them
   eat regular meals.*
   T/F

2. Boyfriends get excited when they hear the can opener.
T/F

3. Boyfriends need the same food at every age and activity level.
T/F

4. Boyfriends will eat anything.
T/F

5. It's possible to train my boyfriend to feed himself.
T/F

The answers:

1. It's true that boyfriends do best when you make them eat regular meals. They enjoy the predictability of a regular feeding time and may have previously experienced too much snacking and chaos in previous living situations.

2. Yes, boyfriends get excited when they hear the can opener. They have a Pavlovian response to the whir of that machine, one of the few household machines they are not afraid of, besides the remote control.

But the canned goods that your boyfriend likes are usually disgusting and inedible—canned spaghetti and mystery meats—and you need to wean him off of these foods and onto something real.

3. No, boyfriends don't need the same food at every age and activity level. Younger and more active boyfriends can get away with hamburgers every day, but an older or more sedentary boyfriend will need to be introduced to fish and other, leaner choices.

4. Yes, boyfriends will eat anything, if they are hungry enough. It's not a pretty sight. Try not to look directly at him if you discover him, late at night, eating condiments with a spoon straight out of the jar.

5. Maybe it's possible to train your boyfriend to feed himself, but it's hard to know for sure. When he's not with you, this is one of the areas of training that fails first. When he's hungry, he'll eat, period.

Shopping with Your Boyfriend and Dressing Him

Your boyfriend may be frightened of the mall. All those unfamiliar people and the complicated levels in the mall and the tough decisions about flared or straight-leg will spook him. Make shopping fun for your boyfriend; don't make it a traumatic experience for him or you'll never get him back there. Or shop for your boyfriend and buy him the kinds of clothes you know he'll look good in.

WARDROBE TRAINING TIPS: BEGINNING, INTERMEDIATE, AND ADVANCED

Now you've got him, you can start dressing him. Here are some tips to make every group of boyfriend, from amateurs to advanced specimens, presentable in every possible situation.

Taking him out
When he looks good, you look good.

Beginning: No matter who he is or what he does, he should own one well-tailored suit—a classic black or gray single-breasted suit. He can wear it to weddings, funerals, nice parties, and to meet your parents.

He should have a dressy white (or blue) shirt that he can wear with the suit or by itself.

He should own one very nice tie in a recent style.

He should own a pair of nice black shoes and a black belt.

Intermediate: If you are taking him to a dressy event, you will want to either be sure he has the "starter" suit described above (and that it has been cleaned and pressed since he wore it to his great-aunt's funeral) if the event is not black tie. He can add a silk pocket handkerchief or perhaps a patterned vest under the jacket to dress it up.

For black- or white-tie events such as weddings, you need to supervise his tux rental. Most men know to avoid ruffles, but be sure that the tie and cummerbund are black—avoid all colors—and that he has the proper dress shoes (which can also be rented).

Advanced: If your boyfriend plans to be out in the evening at formal events on a regular basis, it makes sense for him to invest in his own tuxedo, which will look and fit better than a rented one. The same rules apply in terms of color, but for creativity a vest may be added—it is far more elegant than a cummerbund.

The daily grind
His everyday clothes are usually dictated by his workplace.

Formal office

This is the most difficult workplace to dress for, but your boyfriend can indulge in a variety of lovely suits and shirts.

Beginning: Invest in versatile basics—well-made suits in dark blue, dark brown, and black, paired with solid or patterned shirts. Checked and striped shirts are particularly nice, and men can indulge themselves in candy colors without seemed overdressed. Avoid florals and paisleys.

Intermediate: Moving beyond solid-color suits opens up more dandyfied options, but exposes the inexperienced dresser to danger. Patterned suits should be classic and subtle, with dark plaids and careful attention to choices of shirt and tie to avoid unwanted clashes. There may be difference of opinion about this, but some women find double-breasted and pinstriped suits a little too . . . gangsterish. Care must be taken when choosing and accessorizing them to avoid looking like a Mob lawyer.

Advanced: If he's making some money, handmade suits are key. Help him find a tailor who can cut to fit him. As he becomes a more confident dresser, more fabric options arise: Khaki and seersucker are great for the summer, but linen is tricky and should usually be avoided unless you have servants or are bit players in a Masterpiece Theatre production.

Casual Office

He can get away with nice flat-front chinos, patterned or solid button-down shirts, and nice T-shirts worn under sweaters. (See Casual evenings and weekends, below, for more about these.)

Working "Class"

He gets to wear sturdy jeans, boots, and T-shirts. Yum. So simple, so classic. So hot.

Trendy

Salesmen, hairstylists, and people in the media can get away with lots of black and lots of Paul Smith.

Casual evenings, weekends, and everyday
The boyfriend basics for looking good
on all occasions.

Beginning: For around the house, toss out all of his grimy concert T-shirts left over from college. (He can save one for sentimental reasons.) Plain white T-shirts and jeans are so sexy, and a man can never be too rich or have too many white T-shirts. Keep them fresh and throw them away when they are stained or holey.

Intermediate: Casual pants (jeans, khakis, and chinos) along with polo or rugby shirts, T-shirts, sweaters, and turtlenecks are right for nights out and weekend wear.

Flat-front chinos look more modern and more flattering than pleated-front pants and khakis, but your boyfriend may feel more comfortable in the latter. Try to ease him into the flat fronts. . . .

Jeans should be of a recent provenance, but not too trendy, ripped, or stained. Low-rider trends should be avoided unless you desire "reverse cleavage."

V-necks, crew necks, turtlenecks, and polo necks are the only acceptable kinds of sweater. Boat necks are appropriate only if auditioning for a Jean Genet prison movie.

Buy him sweaters that set off his eyes.

Advanced: Casual sport coats for nice-but-not-formal restaurants and the like can be worn with a T-shirt and sweater for a fresh look. A coat paired with a button-down shirt is fine but might seem too much like office wear.

Turtlenecks might seem a little too European-intellectual, but they can be both casual and formal, they can be worn under suits, and they work with jeans and chinos.

There's something sexy about a cute guy in jeans and a chunky cream-colored turtleneck . . . it's like a cologne ad fantasy.

What They're Wearing, By Group

	LA	NY	Austin	Chicago
HOUNDS	Black linen, Paul Smith suits, Gucci or Prada loafers	Black—Hugo Boss, Armani, Paul Smith suits, Cartier tank watches	Black, with cowboy boots, shearling jackets	Black, with concert T-shirts, black boots
TERRIERS	Pinstriped gray or blue Armani suit, wing tip loafers	Pinstriped, blue or gray Brioni suits, horn-rim spectacles	Three-piece suits with cowboy boots and hats	Sensible pinstripes or gray suit from Brooks Brothers, wing tips, London Fog topcoats
TOYS	Prada and lots of linen, anything slim cut, D&G accessories, huaraches	Gucci, ankle boots, fur coats, Burberry hats, Agnes B., Helmut Lang	Slacker chic meets *Deliverance*, cowboy boots	Ralph Lauren Purple Label, Ugg boots, Calvin Klein underwear

	LA	NY	Austin	Chicago
WORKING	Tommy Hilfiger, Timberland boots	Sportswear lines designed by rap stars	Jeans and cowboy boots, trucker hats.	John Deere caps, Red Wing boots, Carhartt jackets
SPORTING	USC or UCLA sweatshirts, Dockers and sneakers, Abercrombie & Fitch	Patagonia (aka "Panagucci") fleece, Tag Hauer watches	UT or SMU hats and regalia, cowboy boots, wrap-around glasses	Anything with Cubs and Bears on it, Fila, shower shoes
MIXED BREED	Penny loafers, Dockers, Polo shirts, aviator sunglasses, surfer regalia	Steel Seikos, flat-front khakis, Polo or Lacoste shirts, v-neck sweaters	Wranglers, polo shirts, cowboy boots, bolo ties, Tommy Bahama shirts	Gap khakis, polo shirts, sneakers, Top-Siders, Old Navy boxers

You'll let him walk all over you in these . . .

Dress shoes: Four simple rules

1. Black shoes and a black belt are right with almost everything, and you should teach your boyfriend the following rule: He can wear black shoes with a brown suit, but he cannot wear brown shoes with a black suit. This rule is absolute. He can also wear black shoes with a khaki suit.
2. Tan or brown shoes can be worn with jeans and khakis, and light-colored suits.
3. Penny loafers can be worn earnestly or ironically, with or without socks (except with suits), and Top-Siders should only be worn boating or on the weekends at the country house.
4. White dress shoes smack of golf, segregation, and old age, and should be avoided at all costs, unless you are a Southern politician.

Casual shoes: Four simple rules

1. Sneakers are the casual shoe of choice for most men. In general, they are fine with jeans, but sometimes it's nice to break out into handsome casual leather shoes. The danger of wearing white sneakers with everything can be glimpsed on reruns of *Seinfeld*. Jerry wears nothing

else, and it reinforces his Peter Pan image. Grown-ups
sometimes wear real shoes on the weekends.

2. Clogs. Opinion is split on this one. They're comfortable, they're crunchy—their wearer is most likely an
earnest, Earth-loving environmentalist, and if you're dating him in the first place you'll probably love the clogs.
(They're also very European.)

3. Sandals are a popular choice in the summer, and as
long as they aren't worn with socks, are a perfectly
acceptable choice, from Tevas to more expensive ones by
Coach and Prada.

4. Boots are usually sexy—cowboy boots, work boots,
and shoe-boots all have a place in the male wardrobe.
The one exception is lace-up, knee-high black boots,
which mean he's either a Goth or a white supremacist,
both equally unappealing possibilities, unless you like
unfocused rage or remote mountain compounds.

Under it all

Boxers or briefs? This age-old question has been put to
women who have decisively answered: white boxers. They
are the number one choice. They're clean, they're simple,
they don't seem to be expressing anything disturbing. Also
popular are the new boxer-style briefs in dark colors.

Flowered boxers are cute and fun, while briefs with "Mr. Big Stuff" are downright disturbing.

Socks: Like underwear, these should always be bought in multiples so you have plenty—and like underwear, no trying to get an extra day of wear out of them. The best socks for dressy situations are in dark, subtle colors with dignified patterns. The pink-elephant pattern is cute only if you are someone's strange uncle. No white socks for anything but actual athletics or with sneakers, and no dark socks with sneakers.

Accessories can be fun
Beginning: The basics

Ties: Neckties are a great form of expression, and a man should have at least a few to accompany the basic suit, and more if he wears suits on an everyday basis. Bowties are too fey and affected unless he is in a barbershop quartet.

Jewelry: And when we say jewelry, we mean a watch, and later, a wedding ring. Anything else (rings other than wedding rings, I. D. bracelets, St. Christopher medals) is making a statement—and your boyfriend needs to be sure he wants to be making that statement. Rap stars and metal-studded hipsters with thumb rings are excepted from this rule.

Watches: As this is the only jewelry he should be wearing, he's allowed to have a few different styles. But a classic sports watch with a silver band is the best middle-of-the-road-bet if he has only one. It goes with everything.

Leather wallet or a silver money clip: If he's still carrying the contents of his pocket wadded up in a rubber band, it's time to upgrade him. The wallets are classic, while the money clip is more Rat Pack.

Briefcase or messenger bag: He doesn't get to carry a purse, so he has to make due with the acceptable man-bags. Briefcases don't need to match his shoes or suits, but should be simple, dark-colored leather. Messenger bags tell everyone that he's either still a student, works in the tech world, or is actually a bike messenger. Men with issues about growing up often cling to their messenger bags. Let him cling—you have to let him have something.

Advanced: The frills

Cuff links: These are an acceptable, subtle form of expression that are affixed to shirts with French cuffs and worn with both formal and everyday suits. Cuff links are a great gift and always look elegant and sophisticated.

Pocket squares: Like ties, he can use these for a splash of color, but matching them to both the tie and the suit is a tricky, advanced fashion maneuver and should only be carried out by a trained professional.

Vests and suspenders: These accompany more formal suits and can be mixed and matched, but see the warning for pocket squares about the level of fashion difficulty.

Hats: Not the backward baseball kind. Hats for men have gone the way of gloves for women, but occasionally there may be a need for a hat, like the Kentucky Derby or tea with the Queen. . . .

The Other Evening Wear: Pajamas

If your boyfriend is Cary Grant, he will be able to pull off smoking jackets and silk pajamas with ease. However, most mortal boyfriends will need to be weaned off of wearing boxers and ratty T-shirts to bed. (You should set an example by not wearing them either.) Buy him some nice cotton pajama sets in handsome solid prints, and a nice cotton or terry robe. You can even introduce him to slippers!

Don't Let Your Boyfriend Be a Fashion Don't

Sadly, men's magazines don't have that great *Glamour* magazine spread in which fashion offenders' eyes are blocked out with a black bar, while their hideous crimes against fashion are exposed to the world. This is how women are trained about "what not to wear."

No tight pants. He is not, as you will have pointed out to him before, Mick Jagger, living in 1972, or the member of a boy band. Tell him it interferes with his sexual ability when he wears tight pants, and he'll probably loosen up.

Moderation is key. Too much of any particular style is dangerous. If he overdoses on Western, for example, he'll end up looking like one of the Village People.

Dress age-appropriately. Casual is one thing, but we are in danger of looking like a nation of preschoolers in baseball hats, tennis shoes, and jeans all the time. Those clothes are fine for certain things, but dressing up is refreshing—and bold! Also, men over thirty from all races should know they should not dress as rappers or gang-bangers: no baggy pants, no oversize team jerseys. *No ripped or torn clothes.* When it's being held together with ten threads, throw it away. Gentle fraying on a cuff can be aristocratic, but actual holes in shirts or other articles of clothing are unacceptable for anything other than painting the house.

When in doubt, go for simplicity. If your boyfriend is in doubt about whether two patterns match, or what color to buy, the default setting is always pick the simplest thing: one pattern matched with a solid, choosing a neutral instead of a color. Fewer training mistakes will be made, and your boyfriend will look suave and sophisticated.

Concert T-shirts are for home wear. After the age of eighteen, any man still wearing a concert T-shirt out in public is making a statement, one that says "I do not have a day job." Exceptions are made for hipsters (whose day job usually involves record stores and for whom identification with their favorite bands is a deep personal issue), college students, and roadies. You can allow your boyfriend to slip into that Metallica shirt when he's washing the car or wear that tattered Elvis Costello shirt to mow the lawn.

Grooming Basics

Hair: Hairstyles communicate a lot about your boyfriend, and if you got together with a mullet-wearing rocker, don't expect to turn him into a *GQ*-fashionista right away. However, some basics:

Clean It: Hair should be washed at least every other day. Many men will use whatever is available—often, bar soap. Buy them a product that has both shampoo and conditioner, since you can make them use one bottle, but two is asking for too much. Product (mousse, gel, spray) should be kept to a minimum.

Cut It: Long hair on men is for metalheads, men on the cover of romance novels, and people who think it's still 1967. In general, men's hair should be cut in a sensible short cut so you don't really notice it.

Style it: Some styles to embrace or avoid

The Merchant Ivory: Some men have what amounts to pageboy bobs. This works if your boyfriend is British or a fashion model. Otherwise, along with linen suits and bowties, it's a little too fey for every day. The one subcategory of this hairstyle that works on some men is the floppy lock of hair over one eye, à la Hugh Grant. But your boyfriend must be super-cute to pull it off.

The Clooney Caesar Cut: Years after George Clooney abandoned this hairstyle, many others have taken it up, proving that it looked good only on George Clooney. The little fringe is silly on anyone else.

Headbanger's Special: Long and heavily sprayed and sported by rockers everywhere, this one has its fans, and they all live in Jersey.

The Fade: If you're a teenage boy, this is fine, but if not, avoid looking like one.

Dreadlocks: These are attractive on him only if he is actually black. Other men with dreadlocks look strange.

The Cue Ball: Many men with hair problems take the sensible route of shaving it down quite short. This is the right way to go. Very curly hair and baldness can be combated with a short cut. There is nothing as sexy as a freshly shaved neck.

A note on the "Hairless" breed of boyfriend: Many men are worried about their receding hairlines, and invest in implants, plugs, and tortured hairstyles. Although the comb-over seems to be happily dying out, plugs look like a tiny hair farm. If you are the owner of a **Hairless** boyfriend, reassure him that he's still very sexy and encourage him to go with a very short cut. A **Hairless** boyfriend can also experience the fun of hair by having more elaborate facial hair configurations.

A note on going gray and other colors: As your boyfriend ages, he will start to go gray. Never, ever let him touch hair dye. Ever. He can play with highlights if he is a skilled member of the **Toy** breed, but otherwise his hair color should be left alone.

Facial hair: The length and angle of your boyfriend's sideburns is a precise gauge of his hipness quotient. Sideburns are an ever-changing barometer of fashion trends, and most facial hair (goatees, soul patches) is acceptable as long as it does not give you a rash. The one exception is a "Grizzly Adams"–style full beard. An unkempt facial forest does not express the highest standards of personal grooming or style.

Other hairy issues: Most men are very, very hairy. They shed all over everything. Even **Hairless** boyfriends seem to shed. You can stop some of the shedding by introducing very hairy boyfriends to back waxing. And grooming of the hair in the nether regions is also important. Encourage him to trim down there as well (but not wax, which would be weird). As he ages, ear and nose hair also become issues, and you can buy him gadgets to handle those areas.

GOING TO THE GROOMER: IS YOUR BOYFRIEND WILLING?

Some boyfriends may become anxious or obstinate about a trip to the groomer's. Others may go all the time (Toys). Salon visits by men are anecdotally on the rise, and you can sometimes see men getting a pedicure or a facial in big cities. But most men make do with a trip to a barber for a haircut, looking down on men who get their toenails done. However, reassure them that men have been getting manicures for a long time—it's not just an affectation of city dwellers. If they won't go, get them the gadgets that they can use at home.

Put Him on the Scent

The best-smelling boyfriends smell like soap. Sometimes he might want to use cologne, but not too much and nothing too frilly or trendy—the classics like Old Spice are good, or newer scents like Calvin Klein's line are pleasant.

Get Him Grooming Gadgets

Boyfriends love toys and gadgets, and are more likely to groom themselves if you make it fun for them. Here are some of the best ones:

Electric or sonic toothbrushes.

Ion hairdryers in sleek metal designs.

A multipurpose grooming device for nose and ear hair, eyebrows, moustaches, and sideburns. (Don't go crazy on the eyebrows or he'll look like a drag queen.)

A fancy kit with clippers, cuticle scissors, tweezers, lint brush, razor, comb, etc.

An electric clipper for home hair touch-ups.

Razors.

A fog-free shaving mirror.

A waterproof electric shaver.

A waterproof shower radio will encourage him to spend
as much time as possible there.

Troubleshooting Tip #707

The problem: My boyfriend is difficult during bath time:
He hates having his nails clipped, his ears cleaned, etc.

Why he does this: Some boyfriends are happy to stew in
their own filth for days on end, bathing and shaving
infrequently. Proper grooming is anathema to them.

What to do: First of all, make sure your boyfriend
knows that you will not touch him with a ten-foot pole
as long as he persists in his antigrooming stance. Make
bath time fun for your boyfriend. Make sure he is calm
and relaxed. Use bubbles, bath toys, or the promise of
your nudity to entice him into regular grooming habits.

Why this is effective: A creative system of rewards and punishments is always effective in making him see the error of his ways.

How to prevent this: Start this process early in the relationship by making your cleanliness expectations clear. Demystify the bathing process and gradually introduce him to the use of hair products and basic skin care. If you are someone really bothered by poor grooming habits, date **Toys.**

TEN

Going Off-Leash
Introducing Your Boyfriend to Others

Once you have established trust and communication with your boyfriend, you can begin to take him out in public and introduce him to friends as part of his socialization process. In the early stages of your relationship with a boyfriend, it's important to supervise his socialization carefully.

Introducing Him to Your Friends

The first and most important test is what your girlfriends think of him. Getting him ready for that first playdate with your friends involves making sure he is freshly groomed and on his best behavior.

Presumably by this point you and he have reached an understanding about which of his clothes are no-nos (the acid-washed jeans, the pleated corduroys, the man-purse he used to carry) and which are acceptable (the khaki flat-fronts, the black oxfords, and the cute necktie).

Tips for Taking Him Out

Take your boyfriend to an environment in which he will feel comfortable, not anxious.

Taking a big **Working** hunk to a fancy lunch or a fashion show would be a disaster, of course (but a **Toy** would love it!). Your friends will be excited to visit that new sports bar with all the cute guys, and your boyfriend can shine in his own element. Allow the **Terrier** to showcase his knowledge, the **Hound** to slink through the clubs, and the **Sporting** guy to take you all to the batting cage. **Mixed Breeds** will always do what you want them to, from taking you all to a nice restaurant to having a good cry at the movies.

When your friends approach your new boyfriend for the first time, they should do so individually.

Instead of descending upon him in a pack, they should spend time with him individually, and they should not frighten or spook him with too many questions or with inappropriate ones. They should let him warm up to them slowly.

He should be kept on his best behavior around all your friends

No inappropriate sniffing around your girlfriends and no growling or shows of aggression around other males.

Meeting His Friends

Since, as we have noted, many boyfriends are formerly feral, having lived in a pack situation in a fraternity or apartment with other men, meeting his friends may be trying for a new owner. During these early stages of a relationship, you may have the most success in separating your boyfriend from the least desirable elements of his former pack in order to establish yourself as the new alpha dog.

Here are some tactics, by group, for meeting his friends:

Working boyfriends may have bonded to other large men like themselves and probably lived in a very "masculine" world. You will never fit all of them in your apartment, and it's doubtful you will want to spend your time with them watching football in bars or shooting pool, so it's best to try to encourage your **Working** boyfriend to see his friends on his own, once a month or so. This gives him more time to help you with stuff, like moving your furniture, or giving you a backrub with those big strong hands of his.

Your **Toy** boy may also have inhabited an all-male world, but one more connected to the world of decorating or show business. His friends are most useful for recommending the right hair place and taking you shoe shopping. They're all fabulous, but you may find yourself going home alone after a night out with the **Toys.**

Your **Mixed Breed** boyfriend has well-balanced, normal guy friends like him. Nights with them might involve Scrabble matches, popcorn, and down-home fun. You may think longingly of dancing away the night with

Toys in a disco, or making out in the backseat with a **Hound,** but the smart default choice is always a night out with the **Mixed Breed** guy and his affable pack.

A pack of **Terriers** equals a big yapping headache. Try to meet just a few of them in a quiet place, such as a concert hall or a museum, where their warring opinions on everything from acoustics to medieval painting will have to be conducted in a whisper.

A night out with the **Hound** and his friends (you won't get them to go anywhere before at least 8 or 9 p.m.) can be good fun. Just be sure not to indulge in it on a regular basis, or you might find yourself jobless or pregnant or in rehab. And remember, his friends are not a good source of future boyfriends, nor should you set them up with your friends.

Playing games with the **Sporting** boyfriend and his friends can be fun, but it gets a little repetitive after a while. This group never gets tired of chasing this ball or that stick—they can do it for hours, long after your patience has worn out. Best to join in on an occasional basis and introduce your sporting boyfriend to one-on-

one indoor games where his athleticism and energy will be appreciated and enjoyed by you.

1313

Troubleshooting Tip #1313

The problem: Whenever we have guests, my boyfriend is aggressive at first, and then he gets excited and won't stop talking to them and pestering them.

Why he does this: It's natural for him to be possessive at first when someone new comes into his territory; he is protecting his home and his possessions. After he has determined they are not a threat to him, he is excited to see new people and might misbehave by demanding too much attention.

What to do: Set up some visits from friends before a big event so you can practice introducing strangers into the home. Speak in a friendly tone to the guests and make friendly contact, letting your boyfriend know there is no reason for aggression. When he is comfortable with the visitors, keep him calm and prevent him from bothering them too much or from showing them his CD collection. Give him a task like mixing drinks to keep him occupied and happy.

Why this is effective: By acting friendly toward strangers and guests entering the home, you reassure him, and by calming him and distracting him, you prevent him from pestering guests.

How to prevent this: Start exposing your boyfriend to small numbers of guests and work up to bigger groups. Calmly discuss appropriate "party behavior" with your boyfriend so he knows what you expect from him.

ASK
Elizabeth Taylor

Dear Elizabeth: My boyfriend is badly behaved when I take him out into public. He is especially difficult in group situations where he's not the dominant male, and he will start to act out and become aggressive. How do I cure this problem?

Fed Up in Fresno

Elizabeth says: Start by taking your boyfriend out to places where he feels comfortable. For example, socialize with small groups of his friends and reward him with verbal praise when he is polite and well-behaved. Before larger events, speak clearly to him about what dismays you about his unwelcome party behavior and aggressiveness, but keep in mind that some boyfriends are naturally aggressive, and others are naturally insecure about their social position. Assure him that he is the biggest dog in the room and hope he believes it. And watch how much he drinks—boyfriends can get out of hand after a few too many martinis.

Training Outcomes
Breaking Up, or Moving Forward?

The Untrainables:
What to Do When Training Fails

There is a caste of boyfriend known as the Untrainables. Some men, no matter how hard you try, will never be able to conform to your desires or realize the beneficial effects of your training. These boyfriends are usually abandoned by their exasperated owners after about a year or so. They end up sheltering with other cast-off Untrainables or looking for a new and unsuspecting girlfriends and starting the cycle all over again. As Untrainables get older and less cute, it becomes increasingly hard for them to find new owners, unless they have *a lot* of money, but even then a savvy owner comes to understand their limitations and breaks it off. Untrainables may also cycle through younger and younger owners, so by the time they are seventy, they are dating nineteen-year-olds. An experienced woman can spot an Untrainable at one hundred yards.

Trainable, but Not the Right Boyfriend

Some boyfriends are sweet and trainable but end up being incompatible companions. Either you or he may realize this. If he breaks up with you, remember that there are always new boyfriends to adopt. If you need to break up with him, do it respectfully and gently, and try to find him a new owner if you can.

HOW TO BECOME HIS MISTRESS, PERMANENTLY

Do you make his tail wag? Does he want to fetch for you forever? After investing the time and energy to successfully train a boyfriend, it may be time to make the relationship permanent.

Marriage, and the wedding in particular, is the ultimate test of your boyfriend's obedience training—it is in fact both an obedience trial and an endurance trial. A wedding, with its many arcane rituals and its endless numbers of parties and social events, relies upon all of your boyfriend's training. Most boyfriends are not naturally interested in flower selection, napkin color, or meeting your relatives. Only his doglike devotion to you, and his desire to spend his life with you as the leader of his pack, will motivate him to do it.

Involve your boyfriend in the ceremony to the extent that you can, remembering that some boyfriend types are more amenable to the idea. For example, **Toys** will want to help with the flowers, **Terriers** will be interested in choosing the band, and the **Hound** will want to attend all the fittings for the bridesmaids' dresses. Let them participate as they wish, or wish not to. . . .

Good luck!

GLOSSARY

A List of Some Key Terms

Agility trial: Your boyfriend's ability to negotiate a dinner party consisting of your boss, your best friend, and your parents.

Alpha dog: You.

Aptitude: Your boyfriend's natural ability to absorb and follow voice commands.

Associative learning: Method of training a boyfriend by linking an act to a reward. For example, if he shows up on time, he gets to go out with you again.

Big Day: The wedding.

Body language: Physical attitude of a mistress that her boyfriend must carefully learn to read.

Bond: A reciprocal attachment that must be induced before the real training can begin.

Champion: Status achieved by a boyfriend who has completed his training and has accumulated enough rewards to graduate from training to the Big Day.

Cognitive ability: Your boyfriend's capacity to gauge your moods and anticipate your needs.

Dependence: Main trait of the **Toy** breed.

Discipline: Part of training; may involve control, chastisement, punishment, or light bondage.

Dominance training: The wonderful process whereby a man becomes a boyfriend.

Feral: The state of your boyfriend when you first meet him.

Fetch: One of the key commands: slippers, coffee, flowers, it covers so much.

Habituation: A boyfriend can get used to anything.

Imprinting: When a new boyfriend becomes accustomed to your face and comes to consider it to be a new standard of perfection.

Instinct: Must be stamped out at all costs.

Negative reinforcement: Dissuading a boyfriend from incorrect behavior or response to training by scolding or light spanking.

Obedience: The most important trait in a boyfriend.

Olfactory sense: Apparently lacking in many of the male sex. They seem unable to understand when sheets need to be changed or socks need to be washed.

Pack mentality: Trait that must be eradicated: Men must not think like each other, or for themselves, but like you.

Pedigree: In modern terms, your boyfriend's "papers" consist of his MBA, his JD, or his MD.

Pet quality: A boyfriend you might want to date for a while, but not for the long term.

Positive reinforcement: Any reward for proper perform-ance: food, sex, or a new tie.

Punishment: No sex.

Reward: Sex.

Show quality: A boyfriend who has the ability to go the distance, all the way to the Big Day, a.k.a. the wedding.

Socialization: Process by which he learns to love you, your friends, and your family.

Trainability: Another key trait in a boyfriend.

Work-play balance: All work and no play makes him a dull boyfriend.